Berlin

Berlin

By Ryan Levitt

Thomas Cook
Publishing

Published by Thomas Cook Publishing
PO Box 227
The Thomas Cook Business Park
19–21 Coningsby Road
Peterborough
PE3 8XX

E-mail: books@thomascook.com

ISBN: 1841573 647

Text © 2003 Thomas Cook Publishing
Maps © 2003 Thomas Cook Publishing

Head of Publishing: Donald Greig
Project Editor: Jennifer Doherty
Proofreader: Jan Wiltshire

Design and Layout: Studio 183 Ltd
Cover Design and Artwork: Studio 183 Ltd

City maps drawn by: Studio 183 Ltd
Transport maps: Transport Cartographic Service

Scanning: Studio 183 Ltd

Printed and bound in Spain by: Artes Gráficas Elkar, Loiu, Spain

Written and researched by Ryan Levitt
Photography: Gavin Harrison

Additional photography:
Pictures Colour Library: pages 18b, 120 and 122

Cover photographs: Gavin Harrison

Contents

CONTENTS

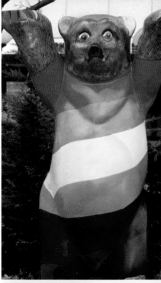

My Kind of Town...

The city of Berlin is like the mythical phoenix, perpetually damaged and rising again from the ashes. Whether due to the effects of World War II or Soviet-era negligence, each new building uncovers hundreds of years of the city's history when construction commences – often to the dismay of everyone involved.

Berlin fascinates me. Always evolving, never stagnant, its residents take on a laissez-faire attitude not found in any other city in the world. As Sally Bowles says in the quintessential Berlin film *Cabaret*, it's all about "divine decadence".

But you can't forget that this divine decadence is what led to the grim years of Adolf Hitler and "National Socialism" that tore the world and this immensely proud nation apart. Berliners would like you to forget that slice of history, but they won't deny its existence if you ask them. While not an excuse for anything, you must remember that Berlin was actually the heart of communist support, ideology, and defence against Hitler's power. During the crucial elections of 1933, Berlin remained staunchly anti-Hitler – a fact that annoyed and ate at Hitler through much of his "reign".

Manuela Roy, the editor of Berlin's premier gay magazine *Siegessäule*, once said to me: "Berlin doesn't have the Western-focused attitude of Köln, the big nightlife of London, the drug scene of Amsterdam or the cosmopolitan fashion sense and style of Paris. But, for some reason we seem to be the most debauched residents of Europe." Politicians politely try to ignore this view, preferring instead to celebrate the fantastic Norman Foster re-designed Reichstag. They promote the city as the newest – and, they hope, soon to be most important – capital of Europe.

So paint your nails green and don't tell mama 'cause you're about to embark on the trip of a decadent lifetime. Maybe this time you'll be lucky.

City of choices . . .

Out in Berlin

Just over a century ago, the first organisation in the world dedicated to equal rights for homosexuals was formed in Berlin, Germany. The year was 1897 and Magnus Hirschfield launched a lifetime's dedication to studies into the "third gender" that would eventually take homosexuality in Germany to a level of prosperity unseen again until the immediate post-Stonewall years of sexual excess. To give you an idea of how far Mr. Hirschfield pushed the boundaries, one can only hint at the levels of scandal that went on behind the walls of his institute during his peak years of research in the early 20th century.

It shouldn't come as a shock that Germany is such a permissive society when it comes to gay rights. Sexual liberation and freedom have been around Deutschland since the division between east and west shortly after the end of World War II. Theorists like to think that this is a result of citizens having had to endure 12 black years of Nazi dictatorship, but I think it's simply because Berliners appreciate and enjoy one of the healthiest attitudes towards sex I have ever encountered.

Berliners take a very "German" view towards sex and regard it as more of a transaction than a romantic culmination. Don't get me wrong, I'm not suggesting that sex between couples isn't a special experience between locals, it just isn't the be-all and end-all of what a Berliner's relationship is all about. If a guy feels horny, he remedies the situation by having sex. Where he has it isn't such a big deal – sauna, kino or darkroom, it doesn't matter – as there's no social stigma attached to a quick pick-up. It's fulfilling a need, after all, and why should there be any harm in that?

Berlin is also probably the only city in the world where the same attitude is embraced by lesbians. They too are starting to reap the rewards of women-only sex parties and orgy nights. There may be fewer nights and events to choose from, but the potential for a luscious night of lust is certainly there.

The peak of homosexual life in Berlin occurred during the 1920s and early 1930s immediately prior to the launch of the Third Reich. The Weimar Republic was a time of fast living and loose morals. A typical night during this time would have seen fashionable icons such as Marlene Dietrich and Christopher Isherwood flocking to clubs like the El Dorado on Motzstrasse to enjoy evenings of excess. Motzstrasse remains the heart of Berlin's western gay community to this day.

This was the era that spawned Isherwood's Sally Bowles, the famed character from his collection of short stories, *Goodbye to Berlin*, and the woman who re-sparked the craze for "divine decadence" (in the

Memorial triangle

form of Liza Minnelli) almost 50 years later in *Cabaret*, the film based on the Bowles character. Isherwood never directly informs the reader of his homosexuality in his work, but the clues are definitely there and were heightened even further in the 1972 film directed by Bob Fosse.

Unfortunately this period of permissiveness was followed by one of the most strikingly homophobic eras of modern history – the Holocaust.

Jews, communists and homosexuals were all despised by the "Master Race". These three segments of society had tended to mix with each other quite freely. Historically, Jews were severely limited in the number of professions available to them. Even when Jews received full equality under German law in the early 20th century, they often remained in their traditional career fields – one of which was the performing arts.

Homosexuals then – as they are today – were also numerous in the worlds of theatre, art, music and design. So Jews and homosexuals bonded, due to common interest and perceived threats to their way of life from outside forces. In fact, some of Germany's most famous

and well-loved performers of the day were both gay and Jewish.

Meanwhile, communists were a well-supported party amongst the intelligentsia. Promising freedom for the workers and a society stripped of racism, sexism and labelling, they were in sympathy with the Jews and homosexuals. The allure, for the Nazis, was all too obvious. Once in power, they lumped all of these hated divisions of society into one group and branded them "degenerates", suitable only for enslavement and eventual mass murder.

In human terms, it is clear that the greatest tragedy of the Holocaust was the sheer number of Jews slaughtered by the Germans between 1933 and 1945. However, historians all too often ignore the number of homosexuals who were killed by the Nazi regime. Lesbians, on the other hand, were almost completely ignored by the Nazis when it came to choosing whom to send to the camps. Lesbianism wasn't considered an actual problem and women were urgently required to populate the land and create the new super-German race that would take over Europe. Often, the "cure" for lesbianism was a quick rape and forced pregnancy to encourage maternal feelings.

The only good thing to rise from this dark period – if one can say this is a good thing – is the creation of the pink triangle as an international symbol for homosexuality. Where Jews had to wear yellow stars to highlight their classless state in German society, gay men were forced to don the pink triangle as their brand. Today, gay rights activists have reclaimed the symbol as one of power, in

Topographie des Terrors

honour of these thousands of murdered victims of Nazi oppression.

Things didn't improve much post-war. In fact, contrary to popular belief, more homosexuals were jailed in the Cold War years than under Hitler.

For once, Germans had the east to thank for positive changes to the law as they beat their western counterparts by providing reforms a full four years before the supposedly free capitalists.

In the early 1970s, the age of consent was equalized by the German government to fourteen. Today, after years of struggle for acceptance and a decade of now defunct right-wing Christian Democrat rule which stifled any attempts to forward equality laws, German gay activists are celebrating success in even more areas of society.

The new millennium brought gay Germans the right to legal domestic partnership. While not quite as groundbreaking as the Dutch laws that allow couples to be formally married, Germany's regulations essentially permit a registered couple all of the rights of a married couple without being able to use the term "marriage". This is pretty much fine with gay Germans as their blunt personalities and straightforward thinking only wanted the opportunity to marry in order to receive the same tax benefits as hetero couples. The fact that they're legally bonded is just a nice plus. And that probably won't stop them from a quick steam at the sauna on their way home anyway.

Much of today's laissez-faire attitude is a direct result of the division of the city between east and west. While the east struggled under the communist regime, the west partied it up under the benevolence of huge tax breaks, subsidised housing and all-night liquor and club laws – the goal of which was to make easterners jealous.

The western powers used West Berlin to showcase the success of "capitalist" structure. Western television was piped into East Berlin homes, exposing many to a luxurious lifestyle they could only dream about. The German government threw millions of marks in tax breaks at the city to encourage employment and production – mostly so that they could flash their success in the eyes of the drooling communists.

The result was a free-for-all of artistic energy, youth, and vibrant freedom. Numerous luminaries, including bisexual singer David Bowie and German punk mistress Nina Hagen, flocked to the city in the late 70s to experience the anarchistic world of what was then the cutting-edge community of Berlin: Kreuzberg. Low taxes and high subsidies combined to keep money in people's pockets and an end-of-the-world party atmosphere buzzing on city streets. This was the era when gay expression and activism reached its peak.

The 80s saw declines for homosexuals, specifically due to the spectre of AIDS that hung over the community. Where other cities shut up sex clubs and went into a long period of chaste celibacy, Berlin went the opposite way, opening numerous hard-core sex "warehouse" events and multi-storey sauna complexes. For gay Berliners, the key was safe sex and not celibacy. Surprisingly, this policy has meant that Berlin experiences AIDS transmission levels that are comparable to other European cities – neither worse nor better than any other large western metropolis.

Unlike Amsterdam, where a poster outlining safe sex policies and a vat of condoms are available at every corner, Berlin's sex establishments tend not to be too pushy. Sex is between you and your partner of the evening and the government has nothing to do with your decision to slip on a condom. Luckily, most people do it anyway.

This anti-government mentality is a common theme in this city. Always strongly left-wing, Berlin is a beacon for free thinkers and will probably continue to be so until its dying day – no matter how much government officials try to transform it.

Today's big gay events, such as the Christopher Street Day Parade, stem from the gay community's battle back from disease in the mid-80s. It could not have been done without the vast numbers of lesbians and gay men who volunteer their time, patiently lobbying the city for support every year. Christopher Street Day Parade is now one of Europe's biggest gay pride celebrations.

In Cold War era East Berlin, things also bubbled as lesbians and gay men met in community centres and halls dotted throughout the city to live their lifestyles and meet like-minded folk. The communist government didn't do much to oppress East Berliners, mostly because they had plenty of other things to worry about (like the constant threat of rebellion, for instance). The secret police (*Stasi*) would most likely have made a note on your personal record about your sexual preferences and would have noted each of your sexual partners during the course of your lifetime – only using the information against you in the event they felt you were getting out of line.

Because of the surreptitious nature of growing up gay in the Eastern Bloc, lesbians and gay men were forced to bond as a community and most eastern gay venues remain fervently mixed to this day. To see the close ties between lesbians and gay men – a rare thing in many major cities – take a wander over to Die Busche in Friedrichshain. It's a real eye-opener.

Spotting your average queer Berliner is no easy feat. Gays and lesbians in this town have managed to assimilate to such a level that the only thing that tends to give them away is a decent fashion sense (Berliners are notorious for having no clue what to wear) and a copy of Siegessäule somewhere on their person. *Siegessäule* is considered to be the listings bible of the city and one shouldn't step outside without a copy. The magazine is available at all gay

venues in addition to many straight bars and clubs – but only the hip ones.

Today, Berlin is queerer than ever. With a gay mayor running the joint – Klaus Wowereit – the rainbow flag seems to be firmly placed on every corner. Before being nominated to take the helm, Wowereit coined what is now the motto for queer Berliners. Refusing to let tabloid journalists out him on the dawn of his election, he proclaimed "I am gay and that's OK" to an awe-struck group of convention-goers in June 2001. It's now one of the hottest T-shirts in town. Be sure to get one in a size slightly small to emphasise your pecs or breasts (depending on which gender you are). Locals won't be impressed – they're just not into that sort of thing – but visiting tourists from the more pretentious parts of the country like Köln and Munich will appreciate your sense of style and knowledge of German politics. The T-shirts also make great gifts.

Bear with us

Filmha

Jeder für sich und Gott gegen alle

MUSEUM BERLIN   ‹FILM MU

House of movie memories

Stepping Out

From the age of empire to the horror of the Holocaust, the sights of Berlin run the gamut. Because of its chequered history, the city holds treasure troves of information and sparkling sightseeing for anyone interested in history, both modern and ancient. If the past isn't your bag, Berlin also has numerous wonderful galleries, museums and landmarks worth the trek. Some of the best are listed below.

My Top Sights

Brandenburger Tor

ⓘ Pariser Platz, Mitte ⏲ 24hrs daily Ⓜ S-Bahn Unter den Linden

The unquestioned symbol of Berlin, the Brandenburg Gate (as it is known in English) has been a beacon for Berliners and Germany as a

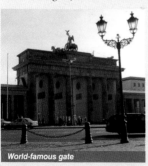
World-famous gate

collective whole since it was placed at the western end of the Unter den Linden in 1791. Once a powerful rallying point for numerous Nazi marches, it was almost destroyed by Allied bombing and communist indifference. It was only after the Wall came down in 1989 that severe damage to the structure was noted. For years, the gate had been sitting in the no-man's land that separated west from east. Following a massive restoration that ended in 2002, Brandenburger Tor is finally back to its pristine self again. (See p. 47.)

Filmmuseum Berlin

ⓘ Potsdamer Strasse 2, Tiergarten 🕿 300 9030 www.filmmuseum-berlin.de
⏲ Tues–Wed, Fri–Sun 10:00am–6:00pm; Thurs 10:00am–8:00pm; closed Mon
Ⓜ U-Bahn/S-Bahn Potsdamer Platz 6 🚫 No credit cards

STEPPING OUT

Before the dawn of the Nazi regime, the German film industry was the leading producer of celluloid extravaganzas this side of the Atlantic. During the silent movie era, Germany rivalled Hollywood in size and scope, producing a number of the big-name stars of the day – including Emil Jannings and Louise Brooks. One of Germany's earliest successes was Fritz Lang's stunning Art Deco masterpiece, *Metropolis*. The museum devotes a large section to this film, along with an overwhelming collection of Marlene Dietrich memorabilia and maquettes displaying early film techniques. Of particular interest is the bittersweet exhibit chronicling the films of the Third Reich and *Triumph of the Will*, the 1936 Olympics documentary work of Leni Riefenstahl. (*See pp.59,64.*)

Gendarmenmarkt

At the heart of the city

ⓘ Gendarmenmarkt, Mitte **⌚** 24hrs daily
Ⓜ U-Bahn Stadtmitte

If there was an acknowledged architectural heart to Berlin, then it would be Gendarmenmarkt. A large square in the centre of Mitte, was built as part of Frederick the Great's majestic plans for his Prussian capital. Home to the breathtaking neoclassical Deutscher Dom church and the French Huguenot Französischer Dom, the Gendarmenmarkt comes alive in summer when the square is awash with street performers, sidewalk cafés and live musicians. It's hard to believe that a mere decade or so ago, many of the buildings in the square had been left to rot, including the Huguenot church which had not been altered since a bomb almost destroyed it in World War II. (*See p.48.*)

Checkpoint star

Haus am Checkpoint Charlie

ⓘ Friedrichstrasse 43–5, Kreuzberg
☎ 253 7250 **⌚** 9:00am–10:00pm daily
Ⓜ U-Bahn Kochstrasse
Ⓥ €7. No credit cards

The Wall may be down but the work of the Haus am Checkpoint Charlie continues. Created shortly after the Wall divided east from west, the Haus am Checkpoint Charlie spent much of the Cold War campaigning for its removal. Today, with that goal achieved, the staff dedicate the exhibits and their work towards chronicling injustice and human oppression by governments around the world – particularly in communist and former communist nations. The exhibit starts in a mood of mild kitsch, with displays showing the various methods used by East German defectors to overcome the Berlin Wall. The tone becomes steadily more hard-hitting and factual as you go higher up the various staircases. (*See pp.31, 36.*)

Moving images

The Jüdisches Museum

ⓘ Lindenstrasse 9–14, Kreuzberg
ⓒ 259 933 or 2599 3333
www.jmberlin.de
✹ 10:00am–8:00pm daily; closed Jewish holidays and Christmas Eve
Ⓤ U-Bahn Hallesches Tor
Ⓥ €5. No credit cards.

No gallery opening has been chronicled with more attention by journalists than the decision to build Daniel Libeskind's Jewish Museum in Berlin in 1989. Opened in 2001, the museum is based around the idea of an exploded Star of David. Visitors begin on the ground floor and work their way up, learning about Jewish history in Germany since the early Middle Ages. As the exhibit continues, the progression into the inevitable begins, as hundreds of stories and images chronicle the effects of the "final solution" on Jewish identity and culture. Be sure not to miss the Holocaust Tower for a quiet moment of heartbreaking contemplation. (*See p.36.*)

Pergamonmuseum

ⓘ Am Kupfergraben, Mitte
ⓒ 2090 5577 www.smb.spk-berlin.de
✹ Tues–Wed, Fri–Sun 10:00am–6:00pm; Thurs 10:00am–10:00pm; closed Mon
Ⓤ U-Bahn/S-Bahn Friedrichstrasse
Ⓥ €6. Free 1st Sun of month. No credit cards

Stony gaze

A trip to the Pergamonmuseum will make you realise that the battles waged on-screen in the Indiana Jones films may not have been as far-fetched as you would like to believe. American, British and German archaeologists were notorious for plundering the treasures of the ancient world and battling each other in their quests for the biggest and best. Where the British went for quantity and quality, the Germans had more of an eye for size and scope – as can be seen in the stunning reconstructions of the jaw-droppingly immense Roman Market Gate of Miletus, the Gate of Ishtar and Babylonian Processional Street and – of course – the Hellenistic Pergamon Altar. Go and be amazed. (*See p. 49.*)

Reichstag

ⓘ Platz der Republik, Tiergarten

🅐 2272 2152

🕙 Dome 8:00am– midnight daily; last entry 10:00pm

🅢 S-Bahn Unter den Linden 🅥 Free

Parliament again

The nation's history can be told within the walls of the Reichstag. Built shortly after Unification (between 1884 and 1894), the Reichstag was burned down by either the Nazis or the communists (depending on which version you believe) on 17 February 1933 – the event that led the Nazi party to assume control over the German government and launch their plans for world war. The new Sir Norman Foster glass dome provides stunning views of Berlin, and the Tiergarten – especially at night – combined with the graffiti scrawled by Russian soldiers in 1945 still visible in the lobby, gives a wonderful picture of Germany both old and new. (*See pp. 62, 66.*)

Imperial pleasure palace

Schloss Charlottenburg

ⓘ Luisenplatz & Spandauer Damm, Charlottenburg 🅐 320 911 www.spsg.ge/F_chab.html 🕙 Old Palace, Tues–Fri 9:00am–5:00pm; Sat–Sun 10:00am–7:00pm, last tour 4:00pm; New Wing, Tues–Fri 10:00am–6:00pm; Sat–Sun 11:00am–6:00pm; New Pavilion, Tues–Sun 10:00am–5:00pm; Mausoleum, Apr–Oct, Tues–Sun; 10:00am–12:00pm; 1:00pm–5:00pm; Belvedere, Apr–Oct, Tues–Sun 10:00am–5:00pm; Nov–Mar, Tues–Fri 12:00pm–4:00pm, Sat–Sun 12:00am–5:00pm; All sections of the palace are closed Mon 🅤 U-Bahn Richard-Wagner-Platz 🅥 Combination tickets €5–€8. No credit cards

Schloss Charlottenburg was never a very important palace for the great Hohenzollerns, but it is the largest surviving palace built by the imperial family. Queen Sophie-Charlotte (wife of King Friedrich I) had the palace built for her pleasure between 1695 and 1699. Used mainly as a summer palace, wings, rooms and apartments were tacked on by subsequent monarchs, transforming the place into a mishmashed collection of sprawl. Go for the gardens and to see the architectural majesty but try not to be annoyed with the German-only descriptions. Avoid any tours, as they take you through some of the more boring rooms in Berlin (dedicated to porcelain and silver – yawn!). (*See p.28.*)

Schwules Museum

ℹ️ Mehringdamm 6, Kreuzberg
📞 693 1172 www.schwulesmuseum.de
🕑 Mon, Wed–Sun 2:00pm–6:00pm;
Tours, Sat 5:00pm; closed Tues
🚇 U-Bahn Mehringdamm
💶 €4. No credit cards

As befits the town that did the most important early work in the study of homosexuality, Berlin has an intriguing Gay Museum dedicated to promoting, studying and exhibiting gay and lesbian culture, art and history. You might be surprised to learn that it's also the only one in the world devoted to this cause. The museum had a much-needed expansion onto the second floor in 2002, but it's the impressive library that shouldn't be missed by anyone interested in queer cultural history. (*See pp.38,39.*)

Gay resources

Garden of delights

Tiergarten

ℹ️ Tiergarten 🕑 24hrs daily 🚇 U-Bahn Hansaplätz, S-Bahn Tiergarten/
Unter den Linden/Bellevue 💶 Free

Berlin's green lungs occupy a vast (167-hectare) chunk in the centre of town, much to the enjoyment of all its residents. On any given sunny day, Berliners will flock to the Tiergarten to make full use of its gardens, monuments, cafés and wooded paths. Speaking of wooded paths, gay men are known for their fondness of these delicately shaded hiking spots – especially in the area immediately behind the Soviet War Memorial. Fans of the archetypal Berlin film, Wim Wenders' *Wings of Desire*, will be familiar with the towering Siegessäule that hovers in the middle of the park. (*See pp.21, 59-67,105.*)

A ruin speaks volumes . .

Around Town

Berlin is huge. In fact it's not only huge, it's really about a dozen separate communities jumbled into one massive sprawl. Divided into a number of districts, each area has its own distinct attributes and residents who swear by their neighbourhood and find few reasons to explore other parts of town. Where Charlottenburg is sophisticated and conservative, Friedrichshain and Prenzlauer Berg are cutting edge and down-at-heel – but in a good way. Bars and clubs in these neighbourhoods tend to take on the characteristics of their surroundings, so once you find a district you like, chances are the gay nightlife in that neighbourhood will also appeal.

Charlottenburg

Once the capital of chic in Berlin, Charlottenburg is no longer the life and soul of the party that it once was. The shopping treasures of Ku'Damm have become decidedly chain-store as of late, and the 70s bunker-style architecture does little to entice tourists with its concrete charm. But that's not to say it should be avoided. Charlottenburg's heyday was fifteen years ago, before the fall of the Wall. This is the neighbourhood that had all of the coolest bars, the best boutiques and the most moneyed folk. As eastern districts opened up to gentrification after 1989, Charlottenburg was left to rot in the hands of suburbanites and conservative folk who hadn't caught up with the mania for all things GDR. Remove any trace of irony or post modern hipness from your person and you'll be sure to enjoy the America-lite trappings on offer.

A DAY OUT

I'm stretching things a little today by getting you to start moving from the world-famous Zoologischer Garten. Technically the zoo is in Tiergarten (*see pp.59–67*), but the main entrance and train station are in Charlottenburg. Most guidebooks and maps will list it in a section on Tiergarten, but I've decided to move it here. Don't hate me for it.

AROUND TOWN

Berlin's zoo is culturally interesting if only because it was one of the first public zoos founded in the world. Pens are a bit small for comfort and it no longer has the leading edge in animal welfare it once had – it doesn't have the space for it – but the aquarium is chock full o' fish even if none of the literature is available in English. It can get a bit frustrating trying to decipher the name of a shark in German. If you want a bit of a lesson in German sex and sexuality (without having to go into any of the numerous saunas around town), drop into the Beate Uhse Erotik Museum. (See p.26.) There ain't much in the way of gay or lesbian artefacts but there are three storeys of historical sex toys and artwork to amuse yourself with. Sweep briefly through the ruins of the Kaiser-Wilhelm–Gedächtniskirche (see p.27) to have a glimpse of what the church looked like pre-war. It's probably Berlin's best anti-war statement, even if non-German readers may find the translations a bit thin. Continue your way along Kurfürstendamm past the shops and glitz, stopping at the Story of Berlin (see p.28) for a bit of local history told interactively. Keep going until you reach Adenauerplatz U-Bahn and go north to Richard-Wagner-Platz. Get out and walk northwest on Otto-Suhr-Allee to explore the Schloss Charlottenburg, Sammlung Berggruen and Ägyptisches Museum. (See p.25.) If you are a fan of gardens and landscape architecture then be sure to allot yourself more time than you think you might need at the Schloss. Return one last time to the S-Bahn at Westend and take it to Olympia Stadion (see p.27), changing lines at Kaiserdamm. Here is where you will find Hitler's architectural salute to the might of the Aryan race. From a distance, the towers that support the Olympic rings look a bit like concentration camp chimneys. It can make for an eerie vision on grey winter mornings. This is where Jesse Owens trashed the Führer's race theories by winning a record haul of four gold medals; where Leni Riefenstahl filmed *Triumph of the Will* to glorify pure-race Aryans and where Germany will host a number of matches for the World Cup in 2006. Listen closely and you may be able to hear the roar of past crowds – either that or the roar of motorcycle engines. The parking lot is often used on weekends by Hell's Angels looking for a convenient place to rev their motors.

Shopping city

☕ Out to Lunch

Dining options in this part of town range everywhere from classy to camp. The ladies who lunch swear by the French-German cuisine of **Bovril**. Lace gloves and a suitable daytime hat are purely optional, but whatever you do, make sure to order one of the to-die-for soups to start your meal. Disco balls, pumping ABBA music and a huge rainbow flag could only mean one thing: you're having currywurst at the **Fritz & Co**. (*see p.93*) stand. Join the various office workers and schoolchildren as they dig into one of the sausage specialities under the yellow awning smack-dab on Wittenbergplatz. Asian dish lovers should head over to **Surya** or **Kuchi** depending on what takes their fancy. Delicate Japanese sushis and miso are available at Kuchi while Surya serves up well-prepared, hot-and-spicy – yet unoriginal–Indian. Dig in!

KUCHI
- ℹ Kantstrasse 30
- ☎ 3150 7815
- ⏰ Mon–Thurs 12:00pm–midnight; Fri-Sun 12:30pm–1:00am
- Ⓤ S-Bahn Savignyplatz
- 🚫 💳 No credit cards

SURYA
- ℹ Grolmannstrasse 22
- ☎ 312 9123
- ⏰ Daily 12:00pm–11:00 pm
- Ⓤ S-Bahn Savignyplatz
- 🚫 💳 No credit cards

Tasty treats

OUTLINES

ÄGYPTISCHES MUSEUM
- ℹ Schlossstrasse 70
- ☎ 3435 7310
- www.smb.spk-berlin.de
- ⏰ Mon–Fri 10:00am–6:00pm; Sat-Sun 11:00am–6:00pm
- Ⓤ U-Bahn Richard-Wagner-Platz
- 💳 €3. No credit cards

The treasures of an empire draw the crowds to this museum just across the street from the massive Schloss Charlottenburg complex. The stunning bust of Nefertiti is the gallery's showpiece item, dating from around 1350 BC, but the rest of the collection isn't exactly chopped liver. Various papyrus items, mummies and other sundry artefacts complete the museum's holdings. Not as inspiring as the British Museum or anything inside Cairo's Egyptian Museum, but certainly worth a look. Try and go as early as possible to avoid the hoards of schoolchildren and granny tour groups. All labelling is in German only.

Remembrance of things sexual

BEATE UHSE EROTIK-MUSEUM

ℹ️ Joachimstaler Strasse 4
📞 886 0666
🕐 9:00am–midnight daily
Ⓜ️ U-Bahn/S-Bahn Zoologischer Garten
💳 €5. V, MC, AmEx

Beate Uhse was a former Luftwaffe pilot, potato-picker and German housewife who made millions out of a post-war craze for marital aids and naughty videos. Located above the Berlin flagship location of her Erotik empire, the museum consists of three floors of artwork and historical articles dedicated to the world of sexual pleasure. Ms. Uhse's Asian collection, consisting of Japanese and Indian prints displaying "foreign" sexual techniques, tends to dominate the exhibition, in addition to a tribute to the now deceased Ms. Uhse that includes some absolutely weird photos of her cavorting with lithe men whilst enjoying the summer Caribbean sun. All in the name of business, I suppose.

KA DE WE

ℹ️ Tauentzienstrasse 21–4
📞 21210
🕐 Mon-Fri 9:30am–8:00pm; Sat 9:00am–4:00pm
Ⓜ️ U-Bahn Wittenbergplatz
💳 Free entrance. V, MC, AmEx, DC for purchases

Five floors of capitalist heaven for shoppers addicted to the world of the department store. Trendy is not really the order of the day. Labels on offer include the standard German fare of Joop!, Hugo Boss and Escada so you won't miss too much if you decide to bypass the clothing departments in favour of the amazing food halls on the fifth floor. Follow your nose out of the lift when you arrive, to enjoy a dazzling array of sausages, cheeses, veggies and anything else you might want to put in your mouth – well almost anything. (*See p70.*)

KAISER-WILHELM GEDÄCHNISKIRCHE

🛈 Breitscheidplatz
🕾 218 5023
www.gedaechtniskirche.com
🕙 9:00am–7:00pm daily
🚇 U-Bahn/S-Bahn Zoologischer Garten
🎫 Free

Once one of Berlin's most active places of worship, the Kaiser-Wilhelm–Gedächnis-kirche was destroyed by Allied bombs during the height of World War II. The church still stands – barely – as a reminder of the effects of war and is in some ways one of Berlin's most powerful symbols of peace. Adjoining the ruined structure is a new church constructed of concrete and blue glass mosaic. It's hardly welcoming architecture but the blue glass does shine brightly after dark,

giving the area an eerie glow. A display showing the church before and after the bombing is on the ground floor of the original structure with German-only descriptions.

KU'DAMM

🛈 Kurfürstendamm
🕾 No phone
🕙 24hrs daily
🚇 U-Bahn Kurfürstendamm 🎫 Free

Ku'Damm, or Kurfürstendamm as it is more properly known, is Charlottenburg's main shopping, sightseeing and entertainment drag. Berlin's Fifth Avenue, it didn't attain its status as Main Street Germany until the city was split down the middle, post-World War II. While the avenue has always been important, politics dictated that West Berlin needed a focus and Ku'Damm became it. The architecture is a bit uninspiring, but it certainly proved to be a hit in 1989 after the fall of the Wall when startled East Germans flocked here to experience copious consumption for the first time in decades.

OLYMPIA STADION

🛈 Olympischer Platz 3
🕾 3006 3430/301 1100
🕙 Exhibition, Wed, Sun 10:00am–6:00pm
🚇 U-Bahn Olympia Stadion (Ost)/S-Bahn Olympia Stadion Exhibition
🎫 €2.50. No credit cards

The stadium of the 1936 Olympics. Jesse Owens stunned and embarrassed Adolf Hitler when he walked – or should I say ran? – away with four gold medals at Berlin's showpiece sporting event. Built in the epic style loved by any good Nazi, the stadium can feel a bit eerie if you visit during the day when there are no sporting events taking place. The desolation is enhanced by the cold lines and towers of the structure, giving it the feel of an urban concentration camp. Remove the Olympic rings from the picture and replace them with the words *Arbeit Macht Frei* to get a taste of what I'm talking about.

SAMMLUNG BERGGRUEN: PICASSO UND SEINE ZEIT

🛈 Schlossstrasse 1
🕾 3269 5811
www.smb.spk-berlin.de
🕙 Tues–Fri 10:00am–

City history

6:00pm; Sat 11:00am–6:00pm

🚇 U-Bahn Richard-Wagner-Platz

🎟 €3. No credit cards

Three floors of art dedicated to the works of Picasso, Klee and Matisse. A few other big names like Cézanne and Giacometti are thrown in for good measure, but only to enable viewers to compare the styles of the day. The collection was put together by art dealer Heinz Berggruen, a noted German art seller who spent much of his life in Paris. The bottom floor focuses on Pablo, floor two is dedicated to Klee, while the top level combines a mishmash of Matisse with a few one-offs. Go only if

this period is a particular favourite (it is for me) but avoid at all costs if modernism isn't your thing.

SCHLOSS CHARLOTTENBURG

ℹ Luisenplatz & Spandauer Damm,

ℹ Charlottenburg

📞 320 911

www.spsg.ge/F_chab.html

🕐 Old Palace, Tues–Fri 9:00am–5:00pm; Sat–Sun 10:00am–7:00pm; last tour 4:00pm; New Wing Tues–Fri 10:00am–6:00pm; Sat–Sun 11:00am–6:00pm; New Pavilion, Tues–Sun 10:00am–5:00pm; Mausoleum, Apr–Oct, Tues–Sun 10:00am–12:00pm, 1:00pm–5:00pm. Belvedere Apr–Oct, Tues–Sun; 10:00am–5:00pm; Tues–Fri 12:00pm–4:00pm; Sat–Sun 12:00am–5:00pm; All sections of the palace are closed Mon.

🚇 U-Bahn Richard-Wagner-Platz

🎟 Combination tickets €5–€8. No credit cards

Schloss Charlottenburg, while impressive due to its size, fails to inspire. Displays are shoddy and uninteresting, tickets to get in are confusing to purchase and the place was only ever really used as a summer playhouse by a few minor nobility. Its importance and interest lies in the fact that it is Berlin's only real royal link to the world of pre-World War Empire. Enjoy the porcelain and the gilt collections – if you must - but spend most of your time in the truly magical gardens. (*See pp.18,19.*)

STORY OF BERLIN

ℹ Kurfürstendamm 207–8

📞 992 010

www.story-of-berlin.de

🕐 10:00am–8:00pm daily, last entry 6:00pm

🚇 U-Bahn Uhlandstrasse

🎟 €9.30. No credit cards

The city's history told through the use of interactive displays, talking headsets and wax mannequin maquettes. Sounds boring? Think again. The Story of Berlin is actually a well-thought-out collection of fascinating snippets of information about the city that takes you from the day of its founding right up to the 21st century. It's a great place to go if the weather turns and you need to kill a few hours inside. Highly recommended.

ZOOLOGISCHER GARTEN AND AQUARIUM

ⓘ Hardenbergplatz 8
☎ 254 010

www.zoo-berlin.de
⏰ Zoo, 9:00am–5:00pm daily; Aquarium, 9:00am–6:00pm daily.
Ⓜ U-Bahn/S-Bahn Zoologischer Garten Zoo
💶 €8. Aquarium €8. Combined admission €13. No credit cards

Zoos may not be your thing and the Berlin zoo will probably not convert your opinions. Small cages, tiny pens and a general lack of enthusiasm display a number of depressed animals in a park-like outdoor setting. Historically, the place is important because it was one of the world's first. Built in 1841, today's park holds more than 14,000 animals and one of Europe's largest number of endangered species. The aquarium is slightly more enjoyable, but you'll need to take a translator. Everything, except the map outlining the workings of their water filtration system, is in German only.

A fishy place

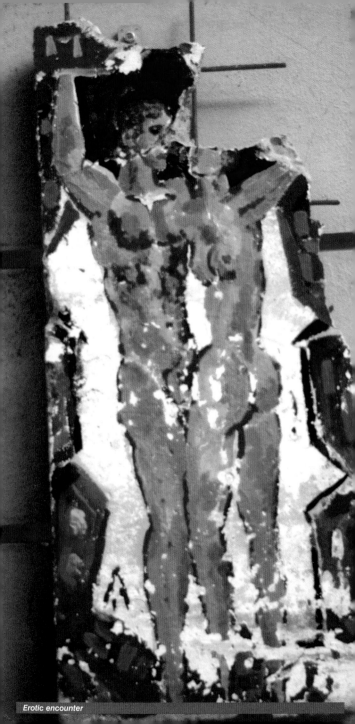
Erotic encounter

Kreuzberg & Schöneberg

Before the fall of the Wall, any hipster, scene queen, blossoming artiste or creative type would have sold their grandmother's left leg to be able to say that they lived in Kreuzberg or Schöneberg. Schöneberg led the two communities in the style stakes, primarily due to its convenient location. This is where Bowie explored his Berlin period, Isherwood created Sally Bowles, where the trendiest gay bars were and the most outrageous nightlife. It was also considered slightly more up-scale than its more down-at-heel neighbour to the east, Kreuzberg.

Kreuzberg more than made up for its less salubrious reputation by hosting the city's massive Turkish population, squatter communities and vibrant punk scene. Left-wing artistic idealism was the heart of Kreuzberg – even if its proponents couldn't exactly see what was going on just over the Wall.

More Chelsea than Lower East Side or Soho rather than Hoxton Square, Schöneberg and Kreuzberg retain a definite gay allure, even if it's only for the sheer number of venues on offer. The choices here can seem slightly mind-boggling.

A DAY OUT

Start your adventure early in the morning at Nollendorfplatz. (*See p.38.*) Home of the Holocaust memorial and historic centre of the gay community, Nollendorfplatz and adjoining Motzstrasse are home to the largest concentration of gay bars and venues in town. Nothing will be open at this hour, but it's a good place to scope out the bars and restaurants you're interested in going to later in the evening. Take the U-Bahn to Mendelssohn-Bartholdy-Park and swing by Grusel Kabinett (*see pp.35,36*) – an eerie Nazi bunker from the war era – and Martin Gropius Bau before making a beeline down Niederkirschner Strasse, with a brief stop at the Topographie des Terrors (*see p.39*) until you reach the Haus am Checkpoint Charlie (*see p.36*). Lovers of Cold War memorabilia will adore the displays dedicated to the Berlin Wall while more political and historical types will be fascinated by the information chronicling the downfall of communism and the methods by which people attained freedom in the west. Go east on Kochstrasse and make a right on Markgrafenstrasse until you hit the Jüdisches Museum (*see p.36*). Taking almost three decades from conception to creation, the Jewish Museum is one of Berlin's must-see monuments – if only for a gander at

Kreuzberg & Schöneberg

ZOOLOGISCHER
GARTEN

Reichpietschufer
Schöneburger Ufer
Schöneburger

Tauentzienstr.

Schillstr.

Kurfürstenstr.

Wittenberg-
pl.

Kleiststr. Nollendorfpl

Potsdamer Str.

Augsburger
Str.

Lietzenburger Str.
Fuggerstr.

Geisbergstr.

Martin-Luther Str

Motzstr.

Bülowstr.

Kurfurstenstr. Gleisdreec

Nollenorfplatz
and Gay
Holocaust Memorial

Bülowstr.

Winterfeldt-str.

Winterfeldt-str.

Kulmer Str.

Viktoria Luise-
Platz

Hohenstaufenstr

Pallasstr.

Elßholzstr.

Potsdamer Str.

Yorcks

Yorckstr.

Fran-ken

Goltzstr.

Barbarossa-platz
Friesinger Str.

Yorckstr.

Eisenacher Str.

Kleistpark

Akazienstr.

Bayerischer
Pl.

Paulus Str.

Badensche Str.

Kolonnen str.

Duden

Martin-Luther Str

Belziger Str.

Rothaus
Schöneberg

Dominicusstr.

Hauptstr.

Feurig Str.

Ebers Str.

Cheruskerstr.

Leberstr.

Nauanstr.

Innsbr.
Platz

Schöneberg

Papestr.

Sachsen-damm

Gotenstr.

Hauptstr.

Friedenau

Voran berger Damm

N

its architecture. Devastating displays and a well-thought-out historical look at Jewish life in Germany from the Middle Ages to modern day have made it a worthy addition to Berlin's collection of landmarks. Head south until you hit Mehringdamm – a great place to stop for lunch or a light snack – and go into one of the world's only museums dedicated to homosexuality, the Schwules Museum (*see pp.38, 39*). Run entirely by volunteers, the museum has an ever-changing collection of work. Keep going south on Mehringdamm until you hit the Flughafen Tempelhof (*see p.39*). Berlin's first airport is significant for two reasons. Not only is it an impeccable example of Nazi-era architecture, it was also home to the Allied Berlin airlift that kept the city out of Soviet control in 1948. At one point during the crisis, goods-loaded bombers were landing on the airfield at a rate of one per minute.

Time to get back on the U-Bahn again for a trip to Görlitzer Bahnhof and the heart of the Turkish community. Market days are the best time to go in order to experience an array of rugs, spices, kebabs and Middle Eastern wares. Same-sex couples travelling together should note that this is not a neighbourhood to show overt displays of affection – you run the risk of harassment. Finally – if you haven't collapsed by now – try and head down to the Museum der Verbotenen Kunst (*see pp.37–38*) and its documentation of the history of the Berlin Wall.

Charlie looks on

Warsch. STr.

SWarsch. STr.

Ostbf.

Museum der
Verbotenen
Kunst

Pushkinallee

Köpenicker Str.

Köpenicker Str.

Schles. Tor

Schlesische Str.

Kulinarische
Delikatessen

GÖRLITZER PARK

Wiener Str.

Pannierstr.

Mariannenstr.

Görlitzer
Bf.

Reichenbergerstr.

Paul-Lincke-Ufer

Sonnen allee

Koltbusser Damm

Hermannpl.

Oranienstr.

H.Heine-Str.

Moritzplatz

Ska-litzer str.

Koltbusser
Tor

Schönleinstr.

Urbanstr.

Südstern

VOLKSPARK

BÖCKLER
PARK

Prinzen str.

Urbanstr.

Alexandrinenstr.

Oranienstr.

Ritterstr.

Jüdisches
Museum

Lindenstr.

Gitschiner Str.

Blücherstr.

Zossener Str.

Gneisenaustr.

Gneisenaustr.

Columbiadamm

Friesenstr.

Haus am
Checkpoint
Charlie

Kochstr.

Kochstr.

Hallesches
Tor

Blücherstr.

Schwules
Museum

Bergmannstr.

Platz
der Luftbr.

Friedrichstrasse

Mehringdamm

Grossbeerkeller

Mehring
damm

Fish & Chips

Mehringdamm

Tempelhof

Sale e Tabacchi

Topographie
Des Terrors

Niederkirchnerstr.

Anhalter Bhf.

Möckernbrücke

Möckernstr.

Möckernstr.

VICTORIA
PARK

Kreuzbergstr.

Potsd Platz

stadt
mitte

Martin
Gropius-Bau

Mendelssohn
Bartholdy
Park

Grusel
Kabinett

Schöneburger str.

Schöneburger Ufer

Gleisdreeck

Yorckstr.

Yorckstr.

Yorckstr.

Katzbachstr.

Dudenstr.

Out to Lunch

If you're a Brit and missing the taste of home, then **Fish & Chips** is the place to go. Mushy peas, malt vinegar and Irish beer combine in this cheap eatery. You won't have trouble finding it – just look for the huge Union Jack. If solid German cuisine is more what you're after, then **Grossbeerkeller** is a better bet. The place will never win any awards for its cooking, but its dishes are hearty, filling and cheap. Try to avoid going at night when the bar-bands come out to play (very badly). Veggies will rejoice at the sight of the **Kulinarische Delikatessen**, which offers Turkish food without any Turkish meat. Aubergine and courgette kebabs are but one of the tasty possibilities on offer. Finally, if something a bit upscale is more what you had in mind, join the hoi polloi at **Sale e Tabacchi**. Artists, musicians, politicians and media darlings descend on this delightful Italian eatery specialising in fish dishes. Be sure to make reservations or arrive early come film festival time. The annual salute to the world of celluloid sees Sale packed to the wee hours.

German dining?

GROSSBEERKELLER
Grossbeerenstrasse 90
251 3064
Mon–Fri 4:00pm– 2:00am; Sat 6:00pm– 2:00am
U-Bahn Möckernbrücke
No credit cards

KULINARISCHE DELIKATESSEN
Oppelner Strasse 4
618 6758
8:00am–2:00am daily
U-Bahn Schleisisches Tor
No credit cards

SALE E TABACCHI
Kochstrasse 18
252 1155
Mon–Fri 9:00am– 2:00am; Sat–Sun 10:00am–2:00am
U-Bahn Kochstrasse
V, MC

FISH & CHIPS
Yorckstrasse 15
0173 867 0130
12:00pm–1:00am daily
U-Bahn Mehringdamm
No credit cards

OUTLINES

GRUSEL KABINETT
Schöneberger Strasse 23A
2655 5546
Mon–Tues, Thurs, Sun 10:00am–7:00pm; Fri 10:00am–8:00pm; Sat 12:00pm–8:00pm
S-Bahn Anhalter Bahnhof
€7. No credit cards

Part historically fascinating Nazi-era bunker, part Halloween-themed scary monster funworld, Grusel Kabinett is popular both with historically-minded tourists and excitable teenagers looking for a shock. Downstairs is where the displays

dedicated to Middle Ages torture techniques and Nazi artefacts are kept, while upstairs is a big, dark scary maze with lots of ghosties and creatures of the night. Basically, it's a melting pot of scary things in one convenient location.

AROUND TOWN

HAUS AM CHECKPOINT CHARLIE

ℹ️ Friedrichstrasse 43–5

📞 253 7250

🕐 9:00am–10:00pm daily

🚇 U-Bahn Kochstrasse

💳 €7. No credit cards

In existence almost from the time the first piece of barbed wire was set down to separate the city, the Haus am Checkpoint Charlie has been acting as Berlin's social and political conscience from its inception. Before the fall of the Wall, the museum was dedicated to providing information about the atrocities happening behind the Iron Curtain, and working towards the Wall's demise. After the fall, the Haus am Checkpoint Charlie went through a bit of an adjustment period. It has now emerged as a wonderful collection of historically significant Wall memorabilia, including information about the ways in which determined protestors and regular folk helped tear it down. The Wall may no longer stand, but the Haus am Checkpoint Charlie's importance and interest remains. (*See p.16*.)

THE JÜDISCHES MUSEUM

ℹ️ Lindenstrasse 9–14

📞 259 933 or 2599 3333
www.jmberlin.de

🕐 10:00am–8:00pm daily, closed Jewish holidays and Christmas Eve

🚇 U-Bahn Hallesches Tor

💳 €5. No credit cards

If you have but one museum in town you can visit, make this the one. When Daniel Libeskind's Jewish Museum was completed in 1998, it was the final step in a journey that first

Libeskind's masterpiece

Gay history

began back in 1971 when the city's Jewish community celebrated its 300th birthday. The Jewish Museum outlines the growth of Judaism in Germany and its importance from the early days of the Middle Ages straight through to modern day. One of the most heartbreaking displays is that of the Weimar Republic. Jews had achieved absolute equality during this seemingly bright period in German Jewish history. The images of cheerful Jewish politicians and families enjoying unheard-of freedoms during this golden age stay in the mind, especially when compared with horrific pictures of freed concentration camp victims. (See p. 17.)

MARTIN-GROPIUS-BAU

🛈 Niederkirchnerstrasse 7
📞 254 860
☀ Opening times vary
🚇 S-Bahn Anhalter Bahnhof
💳 Price varies. V, MC, AmEx

Constantly changing art exhibits are displayed in this massive wedding-cake of a structure named after its original architect. Built in 1881, it's still trying to find its place in the city and is only worth a look if it holds a big touring show at the time of your visit.

MUSEUM DER VERBOTENEN KUNST

🛈 Puschkinallee/Schlesische Strasse, Treptow
📞 229 1645
☀ Wed-Sun 12:00pm–6:00pm
🚇 U-Bahn Schleisisches Tor
💳 Free

AROUND TOWN

Also known as the Museum of Prohibited Art, this gallery is situated in a former Cold War watchtower that stands close to the Kreuzberg-Treptow border. Built around the time of the original construction of the Berlin Wall in 1963, the watchtower has now been transformed into a museum space that holds an exhibition documenting the construction, operation and security measures used to separate east from west. A gallery of art with Wall themes is also on display.

NOLLENDORFPLATZ AND GAY HOLOCAUST MEMORIAL

ⓘ Nollendorfplatz
🚗 No phone 🕐 24hrs daily Ⓤ U-Bahn Nollendorfplatz 🎟 Free

The heart of the gay community, Nollendorfplatz was also the home to the swinging set of the 1930s and the notorious cabaret scene of its day. Christopher Isherwood wonderfully chronicled this neighboorhood in his collection of stories *Goodbye to Berlin*. You can still see his home off the Nollendorfplatz at Nollendorfstrasse 17. Berlin's memorial to the thousands of homosexuals and sexual "deviants" killed by the Nazis can also be found in this pulsing heart of Berlin under the U-Bahn tracks.

SCHWULES MUSEUM

ⓘ Mehringdamm 6
🚗 693 1172
www.schwulesmuseum.de
🕐 Mon, Wed–Sun

Holocaust history

2:00pm–6:00pm; Tours, Sat 5:00pm
🚇 U-Bahn Mehringdamm
💲 €4. No credit cards

Berlin's gay museum celebrated its popularity with a much-needed expansion late in 2002. Its ever-changing exhibits dedicated to queer culture have proven to be a hit with the local populace and are often packed during the museum's limited opening hours. Volunteer operated, staff are eager to please and welcome all interested folk. Be sure to bring academic credentials for a peek at the extensive library of gay and lesbian reading and educational materials on the upper levels (*see p.19*).

TEMPELHOF

🛈 Tempelhofer Damm
📞 0180 5000 186
www.berlin-airport.de
🕐 24hrs daily
🚇 U-Bahn Platz der Luftbrücke
💲 Free

Never has flying felt so dramatic. If Tempelhof's walls could talk, they would speak of German aviation triumphs and tragedies – the Hindenburg, the

Berlin airlift, the Luftwaffe, the list goes on. Originally built in the 1920s, the overwhelming architecture wasn't finalised until the Nazis came to power. The result is a salute to human achievement – specifically Aryan German human achievement – in the air. This is also the airfield where the Berlin airlift helped bring down the Soviet blockade of 1948 that almost defeated western interests in post-World War Berlin.

TOPOGRAPHIE DES TERRORS

🛈 Niederkirchnerstrasse 8
📞 2549 6703
www.topographie.de
🕐 Tues–Sun 10:00am–6:00pm
🚇 U-Bahn/S-Bahn Potsdamer Platz
💲 Free

Site of the former Gestapo headquarters, the Topographie des Terrors stands where the Holocaust was dreamt up and executed by the Nazi regime. Small markers dot the area showing visitors what stood where in the original complex. Be sure to get an English booklet in order to translate the

fascinating displays that chronicle the history of Nazi state-sponsored terror. The entire complex is currently under construction, but remains open throughout the process. A new complex and info centre are due to be completed in 2005.

TÜRKISCHER MARKT AND GÖRLITZER PARK

🛈 Maybachufer/Görlitzer Strasse 📞 No phone.
🕐 Market Tues, Fri early–5:00pm; Park 24hrs daily
🚇 U-Bahn Görlitzer Bahnhof 💲 Free

Home to the fifth-largest urban Turkish population in the world, East Kreuzberg is a buzzy, slightly scuzzy collection of kebab shops, doner takeaways, rug merchants and coffee houses lining the edges of Görlitzer Park. Tuesdays and Fridays are market day when almost every Turk within ten miles of the capital converges on the area in a heaving mass of bartering, buying and barbecuing.

Avoid the area at night and whatever you do, don't display anything overtly "gay".

Atomic clock

MITTE

The historical ground-zero of Berlin, Mitte was for years the heart of Berlin – that is until the Berlin Wall separated it from the west. Mitte's loss as the tony part of town was Charlottenburg's gain until 1989 when Mitte's geographical location drew many a Berliner back to its ancient streets and graceful avenues.

Today, Mitte has regained its status as the pride of Berlin, having transformed itself in less than a decade from a run-down collection of dilapidated buildings to a chic and sleek centre for German sophistication. Here is where you will find Berlin's best shops, finest hotels, famed museums and most important historical landmarks.

Small and compact, it may look like an easy day for the average tourist, but the sheer volume of sights will probably prevent any traveller from managing to cover everything in one day. If you only have a short while, you'll have to rush through a lot of what Mitte has to offer, but it will be worth every possible minute you have available to spend.

A DAY OUT

Begin your day at the Brandenburg Gate (*see pp. 15, 47*) at the eastern end of Tiergarten for your explorations of Mitte. The gate, a symbol of German nationalism, was built over two centuries ago to celebrate Prussian military success and was cut off to westerners for years by the Berlin Wall. Today, it is wonderfully restored and a gleaming symbol of Germany's resurgence as a unified nation. Walk along Unter den Linden, going east until you reach Friedrichstrasse. (*See pp. 47–48.*) Named after the lime trees that were cut down by Hitler to make his military exercises viewable by the German public, the Unter den Linden is one of Berlin's most historically significant streets, boasting more museums and large-scale architecture than any other street in the city.

The walk will take you past the Russian Embassy and the grandeur of the Komische Oper building. Turn right onto Friedrichstrasse – the commercial avenue of Mitte – and enjoy the exclusive shops and services on offer. Stores not to miss include Galeries Lafayette (*see p. 74*), and Quartier 206. (*See p. 71*.)

Go left on Tauben Strasse to take a peek at Gendarmenmarkt. If it's a nice day, this is a great place to stop for lunch and enjoy the streetside entertainment on offer, otherwise explore any of the many churches in the area and backtrack to Unter den Linden, continuing east.

Take this time to explore the museums and sights of the Unter den

Mitte

Reinickerdorfer Str.

U

Hussiten str.

Bernaus

U Schwartz kopffstr.

Chausseestr.

Ackerstrstr.

S Norbt.

Invalidenstr.

Zinnowitzer Str.

U Marcann's

Gartenstr.

Tieckstr.

Torstr

Linie

Heidestr.

Scharnhorststr.

Invalidenstr.

Hannoversche Str.

Luisenstr.

Oranienburger Tor

Oranienburger Str

Au

S Oranie

S LehterStadtbf

Schumannstr.

Reinhardtstr.

Friedrichstr.

Pergamon museum A

Schiffbauerdamm

Am Kupfergra

Friedrichstr.

Willy-Brandt-Str.

S

U Friedrichstr.

Reichstagufer

Dorotheenstr.

Hegel Pl. Str.

Al M

Unter den Linden

Brandenburger Tor

S

Unter den Linden

Friedrichstr.

D H M

Pariser Platz

Behrenstr.

Franz. Str.

Franz. Str

U

Gendarme

Ha

Filmmuseum Berlin

Mohrenstr.

Taubenstr.

Eberstr.

U Mohrenstr.

Stadt-mitte

Leipziger Str.

Leipziger Str.

Potsdamer Platz

U Andy's diner and bar

Krausenstr.

Schützenstr.

Stresemannstr.

Friedrichstr.

Kochstr.

Mend.-Bart. Pk.

U

S Anhalter Bhf.

Kochstr. U

Lindenstr.

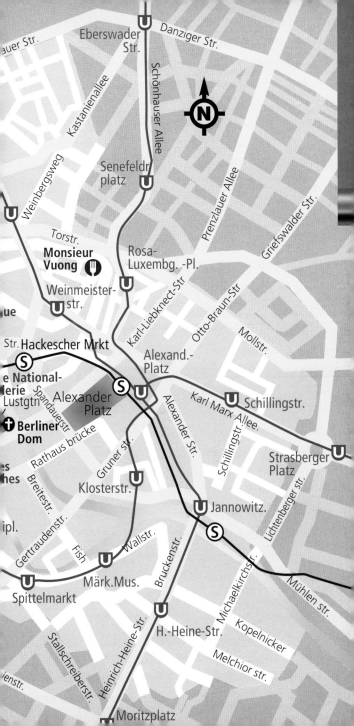

Linden – but be warned, there are a lot of them. Some of the recommended possibilities include the Deutsches Guggenheim, the Deutsches Historisches Museum (*see p.47*), and, when finally renovated and/or destroyed next year (the government hasn't quite figured out what to do with it yet), the massive salute to GDR architecture and design, the Palast der Republik.

When you reach the Berliner Dom (*see p.46*) on your left, go inside to have a peek at Berlin's finest example of church architecture. Keep going up along the Spree to explore the Alte Nationalgalerie (*see pp.45–46*) and its collection of fine art, the Pergamonmuseum with its Greek and Middle Eastern treasures and the Neues Museum.

Take a well-needed break at this point and enjoy a coffee along the banks of the Spree. Busking classical musicians and street sellers palming off old communist paraphernalia dot the area, so it's a nice place to unwind and do some cheap, kitsch shopping.

Cross the Spree on Bode Strasse and continue northeast until you reach Hackesche Höfe. A collection of homes that used to be a stylish Jewish co-op residence, Hackesche Höfe is now a popular entertainment complex with fine dining, theatres and wonderful boutiques. Finish your day with a meal at any of the restaurants in the area and a cocktail at Berlin's most beautiful gay drinking hole, Goldrausch. (*See p.102.*)

Horsing around

Out to Lunch

Bar lunch at Andy's

When it comes to dining, you won't be at a loss for options in Mitte. Ever since the Wall came down, restaurateurs have been eager to take a slice of the tourist pie by opening dozens of eating establishments in the area. Brits missing home will enjoy the faux-English atmosphere of **Astor's**. Options include traditional faves such as Shepherd's Pie and Fish'n'Chips. If you like a little something to look at while you eat, **Monsieur Vuong** may be the place for you. Popular with the toned gay crowd, it also offers surprisingly delicious food. East Asian cuisine is the focus of its varied and tasty menu. For hearty and filling American food in the Potsdamer Platz area, head over to **Andy's** for a burger and fries, while those looking for something a little lighter will appreciate the delicate baked goods and baguettes on offer at **Marcann's** in the north of the district.

ANDY'S DINER AND BAR

ℹ️ Potsdamer Strasse 1
📞 2300 4990
🕐 10:00am–3:30pm daily
Ⓜ U-Bahn/S-Bahn

Potsdamer Platz
💳 🍴
V, MC, AmEx

ASTOR

ℹ️ Oranienburger Strasse 84 📞 283 6834
🕐 Mon–Thurs, Sun 11:00am–1:00am; Fri–Sat 11:00am–2:00am
Ⓜ S-Bahn Hackescher Markt
💳 🍴 No credit cards

MARCANN'S

ℹ️ Invalidenstrasse 112
📞 2832 6171
🕐 Mon–Fri;7:00am–6:00pm; Sat 8:30am–2:00pm
Ⓜ U-Bahn Zinnowitzer Strasse 💳 🍴
No credit cards

MONSIEUR VUONG

ℹ️ Alte Schönhauser Strasse 46 📞 3087 2643
www.monsieurvuong.de
🕐 Mon-Sat 12:00pm–midnight; Sun 4:00pm–midnight Ⓜ U-Bahn Rosa-Luxemburg-Platz
💳 🍴 No credit cards

OUTLINES

ALEXANDERPLATZ

ℹ️ Alexanderplatz
📞 No phone.
🕐 24hrs daily
Ⓜ U-Bahn/S-Bahn Alexanderplatz
💳 Free

If GDR architecture is your thing, then your first stop should be Alexanderplatz. A massive square and communist showpiece, it was also the location of the initial demonstrations in 1989 that eventually served to bring down the communist regime. For a laugh, be sure to keep an eye out for the atomic clock (don't worry, it's so big you'll never miss it), telling time in communist cities around the world.

ALTE NATIONALGALERIE

ℹ️ Bodestrasse 1–3
📞 209 050
www.smb.spk-berlin.de
🕐 Tues-Wed, Fri–Sun 10:00am– 6:00pm; Thurs

10:00am–10:00pm

🚇 S-Bahn Hackescher Markt

💳 €6. No credit cards

19th century art is the speciality of this, the Old National Gallery. A palatial building, complete with sweeping staircases and a wonderful "museumy" feel, the Alte Nationalgalerie consists of almost 500 pieces of important art from across Europe. While the focus is most definitely on German creativity here, the collection also holds important Impressionist works from Manet, Monet and Rodin. Fans of architecture will appreciate the obvious care that went into the building's three-year renovation, completed in December 2001.

ALTES MUSEUM

ℹ️ Lustgarten

📞 209 050

www.smb.spk-berlin.de

🕐 Tues–Sun 10:00am–6:00pm

🚇 S-Bahn Hackescher Markt

💳 €6, free 1st Sun of month. No credit cards

Originally the only museum on the Museumsinsel, the Altes Museum is now primarily known for its temporary exhibitions dedicated to a wide variety of subjects. No longer the most important museum in the area, it is still an admirable structure on this island of architectural jewels.

BERLINER DOM

ℹ️ Lustgarten

📞 2026 9133

www.berliner-dom.de

🕐 1 Apr–30 Sept, Mon–Sat 9:00am–8:00pm; Sun 12:00am–8:00pm; 1 Oct–31 Mar, Mon–Sat 9:00am–7:00pm; Sun 12:00pm–7:00pm

🚇 S-Bahn Hackescher Markt

💳 €5.10. Crypt and cupola €5.10. Crypt only €4.10. No credit cards

Step up to the arts

Glitzy street

Destroyed during World War II, the Berlin Cathedral has finally completed an extensive renovation that has returned it to its former glory. An Italian Renaissance masterpiece, the Berliner Dom sat as a ruin from the end of the war until 1973 when the communists finally decided to rebuild it. For years, the congregation was one of only a few in the world that could boast long-standing members in two separate nations. Some old West Berliner families remained staunchly loyal to the church that was separated from them by politics and concrete. It continues to hold weekly services for devout German Protestants.

BRANDENBURGER TOR

- Pariser Platz
- No phone
- 24hrs daily
- S-Bahn Unter den Linden
- Free

When the Wall came down in 1989, the everlasting symbol that stays in the minds of all who watched the proceedings was the sight of the Brandenburg gate hovering over the cheering masses of newly unified Germans on the Pariser Platz. After the dust settled, however, West Germans quickly saw that the famed symbol of Prussian – and now German – might had been left to rot by the Eastern bloc. Reunification brought a long-term restoration plan that left the gate gleaming following its completion in 2002. (*See pp.15, 41.*)

DEUTSCHES HISTORISCHES MUSEUM

- Unter den Linden 2
- 203 040
- www.dhm.de
- Mon–Tues, Fri–Sun 10:00am–6:00pm; Thurs 10:00am–10:00pm
- U-Bahn/S-Bahn Friedrichstrasse
- Free

Closed until late 2003, the Deutsches Historisches Museum has been benefiting from a much needed facelift that will transform it into one of the highlight museums of the city. No one quite knows what the final results will bring, but the core of the permanent exhibition will focus on specific important eras and dynasties in German history and their relation to Europe and the world in general.

FRIEDRICHSTRASSE

- Friedrichstrasse
- 24hrs daily
- U-Bahn/S-Bahn Friedrichstrasse

Once a pile of chopped up rubble and falling-down property,

Neue Synagogue museum

Friedrichstrasse has finally returned to its pre-war glory days as a buzzing, thriving and sophisticated commercial district in Berlin's historical heart. During separation, Friedrichstrasse was split right down the middle, with West Berlin inheriting the less historically significant southern half and East Berlin getting all of the "good stuff" in the north – a result that annoyed West Berliners to no end. After a decade of renovation, the designer shops, five-star hotels and gourmet restaurants have moved back. If spending hard-earned euros on a few luxuries is your cup of tea, then you'll fit right in.

GENDARMENMARKT

🛈 Gendarmenmarkt
✆ No phone.
☀ 24hrs daily
Ⓜ U-Bahn Stadtmitte
💲 Free

A thriving public square, Gendarmenmarkt explodes with life as soon as the summer sun clears away the winter weather. Lined with fancy eateries and historically important landmarks, Gendarmenmarkt was built to tie in with Frederick the Great's vision of a capital city to match his grandiose plans for Prussia. One look at the scale of what was completed and you won't wonder why the Prussian empire was as important as it once was.

If mimes, flute players and wacky jugglers leave you cold, you might want to avoid the place on weekends. (*See p. 16.*)

NEUE SYNAGOGUE

🛈 Oranienburger Strasse 28–30
✆ 8802 8316
www.cjudaicum.de
☀ Sept–Apr, Mon–Thurs, Sun 10:00am–6:00pm; Fri 10:00am–2:00pm;

May–Aug, Sun–Mon
10:00am–8:00pm;
Tues–Thurs
10:00am–6:00pm; Fri
10:00am–5:00pm
€3 No credit cards

No longer a working synagogue – Allied bombing in 1945 can be thanked for that – the Neue Synagogue remains as a symbol of the shattered past of Berlin's Jewish community.

Once a thriving temple, the synagogue was built between 1857 and 1866 and inaugurated in the presence of Bismarck. The beginning of the end arrived when the building was targeted by Nazis on Kristallnacht in 1938. Today, an exhibition about Jewish life and the remains of the structure remind today's travellers of yesterday's tragedies.

PERGAMONMUSEUM

Am Kupfergraben
2090 5577
www.smb.spk-berlin.de
Tues–Wed, Fri–Sun
10:00am–6:00pm; Thurs
10:00am–10:00pm; Mon
closed
U-Bahn/S-Bahn
Friedrichstrasse
€6, free 1st Sun of
month. No credit cards

Named after the massive Hellenistic Pergamon Altar it houses inside, the Pergamonmuseum is Berlin's answer to the British Museum – a vast collection of Greek and Islamic treasures plundered by past explorers for the whims of the public. Okay, so it isn't exactly politically correct, but the exhibits are stunning. The room housing the Pergamon Altar alone is about the size of a small football pitch – and that's not even including the museum's two other highlights, the Roman Gate of Miletus and the Babylonian Gate of Ishtar (see pp. 17, 18).

Statue with a six pack

Anyone for the Planetarium?

Prenzlauer Berg & Friedrichshain

Yesterday's slums are tomorrow's palaces – and if you don't believe that then come on down to Prenzlauer Berg and Friedrichshain. Sassy dot.com types and thirty-something millionaires are flocking to the genteel (and cheap) homes of these two former East German neighbourhoods, transforming them into the hottest parts of town. As Charlottenburg sinks into the mire of its own pretensions and Kreuzberg loses its once avant-garde lustre, Prenzl'berg and Friedrichshain are cleaning up. If you consider yourself to be on-the-edge, up-to-the-minute and in-the-know, then this is the part of town you're going to want to stick to for the bulk of your holiday. Birthplace of the East Berlin dissident movement (in Kollwitzplatz) and home to the continued support of communist culture (on Karl-Marx-Allee), these neighbourhoods are famed for their heated street-corner ideological discussions and debates – preferably in one of the district's more fashionable cafés. You wouldn't want to freeze while defending the merits of communism now, would you?

A DAY OUT

Getting around these two neighbourhoods can become a bit of an epic journey, mostly because they cover large chunks of the central-eastern parts of the city. Begin your day early at Schönhauser Allee U-Bahn station and head westbound towards the Vitra Design Museum. (See p.57.) A showpiece for temporary exhibits on some of the design world's more adventurous artists, its displays can be hit or miss depending on what they have on tap. Continue south on Schönhauser Allee, stopping briefly at the Kulturbrauerei, and continue southeast down Knaackstrasse until you reach Kollwitzplatz (see p.56), the Synagoge Rykestrasse and the Wasserturm. (See p.57.) Kollwitzplatz is a nice possibility for lunch, so take the time to look around, especially at the original home of anti-communist sentiment the Café Westphal (now a Greek restaurant). It was in this tiny bôite's confines that the original seeds for overthrowing the government were planted in the minds of disgruntled East Berliners.

Architecture lovers should go north on Husemannstrasse to take a look at one of the area's nicest collection of homes, renovated back in 1987 by the GDR government to celebrate the 750th anniversary of the city. It was one of East Berlin's specially selected streets honoured with such treatment – although many argue the actual work was completely botched. Judge for yourself.

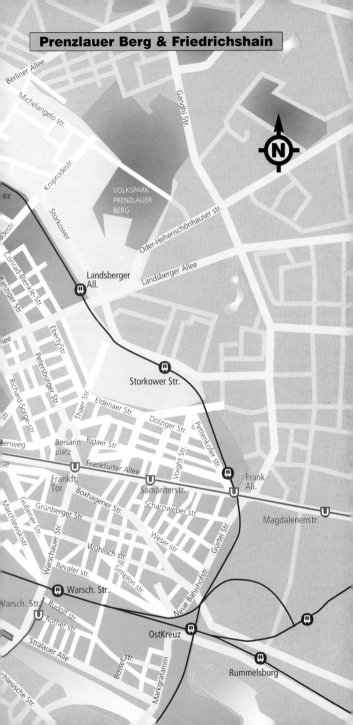

Continue along Knaackstrasse until you reach Prenzlauer Allee. Astro-fans should turn left and follow Prenzlauer until you reach the Zeiss-Grossplanetarium. (*See p.57*). Otherwise, cross Prenzlauer Allee and Knaackstrasse renames itself as Immanuelkirchstrasse. Continue along in this direction, following any roads that go the same way, until you hit the Volkspark Friedrichshain. (*See p.57*).

The Volkspark is Friedrichshain's crowning glory, beloved by all of its residents. Entire streets empty onto the welcoming pathways in summer and entire gay bars end up hovering in the bushes after dark. It all depends on what sort of exercise you're looking to get. If you need a break at this point, the café in the centre of the park is a popular spot for a quick drink amongst the neighbourhood's gay populace. It's good for a cup of tea and a few ganders at the local crumpet. Go south on Lichtenberger Strasse away from the Volkspark once you've had your fill of greenery and continue towards the northern banks of the Spree, stopping halfway at Karl-Marx-Allee (*see p.56*) to admire the grandeur of the street's GDR-era buildings and structures.

Once you arrive at the Spree on Holzmarktstrasse, turn left until it renames itself as Mühlenstrasse. The East Side Gallery (*see p.55*) and its segment of original Berlin Wall should be on your right. Take a peek at the artistically inspiring offerings and end your day by collapsing in the first bar possible. You've earned a much needed drink by now – either that or an expensive taxi ride straight back to your hotel room.

Stop at the old brewery

Out to Lunch

GUGELHOF

Alsatian tidbits

Gugelhof is the widely acknowledged restaurant that launched Prenzlauer Berg into the big-time dining stakes. Its Alsatian cuisine is highly regarded citywide. Those wishing for good food at a slightly lower cost should tuck into the budget French cuisine at **Bistro Chez Maurice**. The surroundings may be slightly down-at-heel but the food certainly isn't. Whatever you do, you can't leave the neighbourhood without a quick bite at a local Imbiss. For the best currywurst in town, **Konnopke's** is the unbeatable choice, while fans of falafel should head over to **Safran**. Political discussion with the mightily opinionated locals is a part of the flavour of any Imbiss in this quarter of town. Travellers are welcome to join-in with the heated discussions as long as they speak fluent German and their views match the local populace. English-speaking Republicans and Conservatives are well advised to keep their opinions to themselves.

BISTRO CHEZ MAURICE

🛈 Bötzowstrasse 39
📞 4280 4723
🕐 12:00pm–midnight daily
🚇 S-Bahn Greifswalder Strasse 💳 💳
No credit cards

GUGELHOF

🛈 Knaackstrasse 37
📞 442 9229
🕐 10:00am–1:00am daily
🚇 U-Bahn Senefelderplatz
💳 💳
V, MC, AmEx

KONNOPKE'S IMBISS

🛈 Corner of Danziger Strasse/Schönhauser Allee
📞 No phone.
🕐 Mon–Sat 5:00am–7:00pm
🚇 U-Bahn Eberswalder Strasse
💳 💳
No credit cards

SAFRAN

🛈 Knaackstrasse 14
📞 No phone
🕐 Mon–Fri, Sun 11:00am–1:00am; Sat 11:00am–3:00am
🚇 U-Bahn Senefelderplatz
💳 💳
No credit cards

OUTLINES

EAST SIDE GALLERY

🛈 Mühlenstrasse
📞 No phone.
🕐 24hrs daily
🚇 U-Bahn Warschauer Strasse 💳 Free

One of the few remaining stretches of the Berlin Wall still left on display – and not boxed up and sold as Christmas stocking stuffers in 1989 – the East Side Gallery is now a showpiece for international artists. All of the artwork is dedicated to the promotion of peace. While not the only place to see a bit of original Wall, it is certainly one of the larger chunks available.

HUSEMANNSTRASSE

- 🛈 Husemannstrasse
- 📞 No phone
- ⏰ 24hrs daily
- Ⓤ U-Bahn Eberswalder Strasse
- 💲 Free

A pretty little avenue, running just off Kollwitzplatz, it was renovated and restored (badly) by the East German government in 1987 to celebrate the 750th anniversary of Berlin. A quick once-over of the street is much more satisfying than any detailed examination of the various homes with their cracks and flaking plaster.

KARL-MARX-ALLEE

- 🛈 Karl-Marx-Allee
- 📞 No phone.
- ⏰ 24hrs daily
- Ⓤ U-Bahn/S-Bahn Alexanderplatz
- 💲 Free

Once the showpiece street of East Berlin, Karl-Marx-Allee is now one of Berlin's hippest addresses, thanks largely to the current vogue for anything GDR. Massive in size, Karl-Marx-Allee was made to impress, requiring a 90metre walk merely to cross it. The street is dotted with Soviet-style architecture and "workers' palaces" constructed from the rubble of World War II buildings. Ironic, considering that this is the street the Russians fought down when battling to capture Berlin in 1945.

KOLLWITZPLATZ

- 🛈 Kollwitzplatz
- 📞 No phone
- ⏰ 24hrs daily
- Ⓤ U-Bahn Senefelderplatz
- 💲 Free

The centre of the buzzing Prenzlauer Berg action, Kollwitzplatz is a pretty collection of cafés, pubs, restaurants and shops named after early 20th century progressive graphic artist Käthe Kollwitz. It was in this little square that the first seeds of anti-communist rebellion began when dissidents met in the Café Westphal in the early 1980s. It is now a Greek restaurant. An organic wholefoods market is held in Kollwitzplatz every Thursday.

KULTURBRAUEREI

- 🛈 Knaackstrasse
- 📞 No phone.
- ⏰ 8:30am–midnight daily
- Ⓤ U-Bahn Eberswalder Strasse 💲 Free

A brewery turned shopping mall with a collection of galleries, boutiques, restaurants and cafés. Popular with the local crowd and

Monument to style

window shoppers. The entire complex can get very busy on weekends and after dark. Recommended, if only to pass a few rainy or snow-swept hours.

SYNAGOGE RYKESTRASSE

- 🛈 Rykestrasse
- ☎ No phone
- ☀ Hours vary depending on holidays and services. Closed to public Friday evenings and all day Saturdays.
- Ⓤ U-Bahn Senefelderplatz
- 🎟 Free

Once the only working synagogue in East Berlin, the Synagoge Rykestrasse was badly damaged during Kristallnacht in 1938. Left to rot by the Soviets until 1953, it is now the neighbourhood's Jewish place of worship.

VITRA DESIGN MUSEUM

- 🛈 Kopenhagener Strasse 58
- ☎ 473 7770
- www.design-museum.de
- ☀ Tues–Thurs, Sat–Sun 11:00am–8:00pm; Fri 11:00am–10:00pm
- Ⓤ U-Bahn/S-Bahn Schönhauser Allee
- 🎟 €5.50. V, MC, AmEx

Temporary and sometimes truly awful exhibits based around

themes or the work of individuals. Displays can vary between conceptual art, architecture and design, but the final result is always intended to inform and question. Often hit or miss.

VOLKSPARK FRIEDRICHSCHAIN

- 🛈 Friedenstrasse
- ☎ No phone.
- ☀ 24hrs daily
- Ⓤ U-Bahn Schilling-Strasse
- 🎟 Free

The green lungs of this largely industrial neighbourhood, the Volkspark Friedrichshain is exactly what its name says it is – a park for all the people. Warm summer days transform the public greenspace into a teeming mass of largely lower-to–middle class families – a reflection of the area's residents. Socialist art and fairytale characters litter the lawns, making it slightly eerie after dark when the local gay community comes out to play.

WASSERTURM

- 🛈 Knaackstrasse
- ☎ No phone.
- ☀ 24hrs daily
- Ⓤ U-Bahn Senefelderplatz
- 🎟 Free

Not exactly a stop to plan your whole vacation around, Wasserturm is more of a neighbourhood landmark rather than anything else. A circular water tower built between 1852 and 1875, Wasserturm provided Germany with its first-ever source of domestic running water. Unless you're a real fan of this sort of thing, stop briefly, point the camera and move on.

ZEISS-GROSS-PLANETARIUM

- 🛈 Prenzlauer Allee 80
- ☎ 4218 4512
- www.astw.de
- ☀ Mon–Fri 8:00am–12:00pm, 1:00pm–3:00pm
- Ⓤ S-Bahn Prenzlauer Allee
- 🎟 Varies. No credit cards

Every city has one and Berlin is no exception. Germany's capital planetarium is smack-dab in the heart of Berlin's trendiest neighbourhood. Seeing stars has never been easier – and we do mean the kind in the sky. A new complex as far as planetariums go, the place is fitted with state-of-the-art equipment. Unfortunately, the exhibits are only in German.

Perfect garden of tranquility

Tiergarten

Every major European city has its major park. Paris has the
Bois de Boulogne, London boasts Hyde Park and Berlin has its
Tiergarten. Originally a hunting ground, the Tiergarten
stretches between some of Berlin's most historically significant
structures, moving east to west from the Brandenburg Gate to
the Zoologischer Garten. The war almost destroyed Tiergarten,
with rumours of civilians eating the zoo's exotic animals and
chopping down the vast forests for use as firewood proving
quite true. Today, Tiergarten is a beloved hub of outdoor
pursuits, including a notorious gay cruising ground that could
rival even London's Hampstead Heath in scope and size.
Ironically enough, it's located right behind the Soviet War
Memorial. Summer days may be the most logical time to
explore the area, but winter strolls have an attraction in their
own right. The wooded lanes blanketed under a layer of snow
can provide some of the most romantic moments of any trip,
especially if you make use of some of the alternative methods
of transportation, including rickshaws and horse-drawn
carriages.

A DAY OUT

Tiergarten is not an easy walk in the park. The greenspace covers over
412 acres in the heart of the city and it would be almost impossible to
examine every piece of flora and fauna in the vicinity. Begin your stroll in
the newly transformed Potsdamer Platz. Once a no-man's-land of
desolation created by the Berlin Wall, Potsdamer Platz has regained its
mantle as the heart of Berlin after a decade-long construction project that
has re-paved, glassed-over and Americanised the collection of skyscrapers
that make the place what it is. If you're looking for a burger, a bit of
shopping-mall culture and a blockbuster Hollywood film in English, then
this is the place to go. Art lovers should be sure to hit Sammlung
DaimlerChrysler (*see p.66*) for its collection of modern work. Other
hotspots in the area are the incomparable Filmmuseum Berlin (*see pp.
15,64*) with its wonderful collection of 30s German film and Marlene
Dietrich memorabilia, the Neue Nationalgalerie (*see p.66*) dedicated to
work from the 20th century and the Gemäldegalerie collection of top
European paintings. Continue along Reichpietschuferm, being sure not
to miss the Gedenkstätte Deutscher Widerstand (Memorial of the
German Resistance) (*see p.65*) and its exhibit chronicling domestic
resistance to Nazism, until you get to the Bauhaus-Archiv. Architecture
and design devotees should rest here awhile, otherwise turn right up
Klingelhöferstrasse and begin your journey through the Tiergarten.

AROUND TOWN

Up ahead should be the triumphal column known as the Siegessäule. Fans of the Wim Wenders film *Wings of Desire* will recognise the structure immediately as the spot where angels watch over the citizens below. Siegessäule (*see p. 67*) also gives its name to Berlin's most important gay and lesbian city magazine – largely due to its resemblance to a piece of male anatomy. Stop off for a well-deserved coffee at the Café am Neuen See on Lichtensteinallee. It's the best place in the park to soak in the view of the gardens and indulge in a bit of people-watching.

When you're ready, meander your way through some of the trails, being sure to go in an easterly direction as you do so. Pass by the Haus der Kulturen den Welt (*see p. 65*) to see if there are any exhibits of interest, and then check out the Soviet War Memorial (or perhaps what's going on behind it if it happens to be dark by this time) and enter the German parliament buildings – the Reichstag (*see p. 66*). Old and new meet harmoniously in this grand edifice that acts as a living reminder of Germany's past. Graffiti scrawled by Soviet soldiers as they conquered the capital remains in the sunlight-drenched lobby, compliments of the Sir Norman Foster glass dome that provides some of the best views of the city – especially after the sun goes down.

A clear perspective

Out to Lunch

As the district of Tiergarten is largely parkland, the opportunities for culinary pleasure are decidedly limited. **Café Nola** is a nice possibility for those wanting American food – but not burgers and chips. Light Californian is the focus, with lots of avocado, mango and salads on offer to the adoring masses. Grilled fish and spiced chicken are the dishes of choice at **Casa Portuguesa** – and well worth the walk to the out-of-the-way corner of Berlin this restaurant is situated on. The unique **Spätzle** pastas of Germany are the speciality of the restaurant of the same name. Served with traditional bratwurst and dark German brews, a stop here makes for a filling meal. Meanwhile, a walk into **Tiergarten Quelle** may result in an inability to stumble out. Cheap beer, even cheaper food and a rough-at-the-edges atmosphere make this place a popular student hangout, complete with chipped wooden chairs and sawdust on the floor. Try to avoid the puddles of vomit at weekends. It's harder than you might think.

Basic dining but tranquil surroundings

CAFÉ NOLA

Dortmunder Strasse 9
399 6969
www.nola.de
Mon–Sat
4:00pm–1:00am; Sun;
10:00am–1:00am
U-Bahn Hansaplatz
V, MC, AmEx

CASA PORTUGUESA

Helmholtzstrasse 15
393 5506
6:00pm–1:00am daily
U-Bahn Turmstrasse
No credit cards

SPÄTZLE

Luneberger Strasse 390
No phone.
Mon–Sat
9:00am–8:00pm; Sun
11:00am–8:00pm
S-Bahn Bellevue
No credit cards

TIERGARTEN QUELLE

Stadtbahnbogen 482
392 7615
Mon–Fri
4:00pm–midnight;
Sat–Sun 12:00pm–
1:00am
S-Bahn Tiergarten
No credit cards

OUTLINES

BAUHAUS MUSEUM

ℹ️ Klingelhöferstrasse 13–14

📞 254 0020

🕐 Mon, Wed–Sun 10:00am–5:00pm 🚇 U-Bahn Nollendorfplatz

🎟️ €4. No credit cards

The work of the Bauhaus design movement is the focus of this single-storey museum housed in a building originally designed by Walter Gropius, the founder of the movement. Sculpture, furniture, artwork and sketches from the hands of Bauhaus designers fill the gallery space, showcasing the German movement that reached its climax between 1919 and 1933. The Nazis closed the centre down when they came to power due to the perceived degeneracy of the school's output. A permanent collection is always on offer in addition to the constantly changing temporary showcases.

TIERGARTEN

ℹ️ Tiergarten

📞 No phone.

🕐 24hrs daily

🚇 U-Bahn Hansaplätz, S-Bahn Tiergarten/

Bauhaus blocks

Unter den Linden/Bellevue

🎟️ Free

Berlin's rural heart beckons one and all to its sprawling mass of wooded parkland, winding trails and luscious lakes. Hiking, biking, boarding and cruising can be found here at any time of day depending on where in the park you find yourself and what the temperature outside happens to be. Warm summer days bring office workers outside where they can enjoy a picnic lunch and the luxury of stripping off totally naked for an hour of sun worshipping. Because of its size, Tiergarten never feels too crowded, so you should be able to find a place for solitude on even the busiest of weekends. (See p.19.)

FILMMUSEUM BERLIN

ℹ️ Potsdamer Strasse 2,

🚇 Tiergarten

📞 300 9030

🌐 www.filmmuseum–berlin.de

🕐 Tues–Wed, Fri–Sun 10:00am–6:00pm; Thurs 10:00am–8:00pm; closed Mon

U-Bahn/S-Bahn Potsdamer Platz

🎟️ €6. No credit cards

German film from the dawn of the celluloid era to today is what's on offer at the fabulous Filmmuseum Berlin. Located in a sparkling new structure on Potsdamer Platz, the ride in the lift to the main doors is enough to leave you awe-struck – and that's before you see any of the exhibits. Displays show everything from early film cameras to scenes from the recent German hit *Run Lola*

Run. Be sure not to miss the sections chronicling Marlene Dietrich, the film *Metropolis*, the use of film in Nazi propaganda and the work of document-arian Leni Riefenstahl. (*See pp. 15, 16.*)

GEDENKSTÄTTE DEUTSCHER WIDERSTAND

🛈 Stauffenbergstrasse 13–14

📞 2699 5000

www.gdw-berlin.de

🕙 Mon–Wed, Fri 9:00am–6:00pm; Thurs, Sat–Sun 10:00am–6:00pm

🚇 U-Bahn Kurfürstenstrasse

🎟 Free

It's hard to remember that Nazi Germany had both collaborators and resisters. Too little is ever said about the brave individuals inside the Third Reich who attempted to fight back against the curse of National Socialism. Gedenkstätte Deutscher Widerstand attempts to right these wrongs with a memorial and exhibition dedicated to German resistance. It was at this site that a group of conspirators attempted to assassinate Hitler on 20 July 1944. A plaque at the rear of the building shows you

the exact spot where it happened.

GEMÄLDEGALERIE

🛈 Matthäikirchplatz 8

📞 266 2951

🕙 Tues–Wed, Fri–Sun 10:00am–6:00pm; Thurs 10:00am–8:00pm

🚇 U-Bahn/S-Bahn Potsdamer Platz

🎟 €3. No credit cards

Early European paintings are displayed gloriously in the Gemäldegalerie. Rooms are separated by both region and period, giving gallery-goers a wonderful opportunity to examine the changing fads and fashions of European art from the Middle Ages to the 18th century. While most of the big names are represented, Rembrandt fans will be particularly happy – the gallery owns about

20 masterpieces.

HAUS DER KULTUREN DER WELT

🛈 John-Foster-Dulles-Allee 10

📞 397 870

🕙 Tues–Sun 9:00am–9:00pm

🚇 S-Bahn Bellevue

🎟 Price varies. No credit cards

The "House of World Cultures" was established in 1989 to promote artists and work from developing countries. The result is an ever-changing and often popular mix of temporary exhibits dedicated to spectaculars from every far-flung corner of the globe. Film screenings, lectures, performances and discussions are held on a regular basis and often prove to be the hottest ticket in town.

Time for the flicks

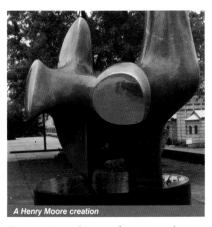
A Henry Moore creation

Go expecting nothing and the place might just prove to be a highlight to your trip.

NEUE NATIONALGALERIE

🛈 Potsdamer Strasse 50

📞 266 2662

☀ Tues–Wed 10:00am–6:00pm; Thurs 10:00am–10:00pm; Fri 10:00am–8:00pm; Sat–Sun 11:00am–8:00pm

Ⓜ U-Bahn/S-Bahn Potsdamer Platz

💳 €3. No credit cards

Just down the street from the Gemäldegalerie, the Neue Nationalgalerie brings art into the 20th century with a wonderful collection of modern work with a decidedly German focus. Entering the vast museum may feel like you've just gone into some bizarre bank lobby – thanks to the often sparse and underwhelming 60s architecture of Mies van der Rohe – but the collection of work in the basement, including a large number of paintings from Otto Dix, make it worth the trip.

REICHSTAG

🛈 Platz der Republik

📞 2272 2152

☀ Dome 8:00am–midnight daily; last entry 10:00pm

Ⓜ S-Bahn Unter den Linden

💳 Free

In terms of modern Berlin history, no structure holds more significance than the Reichstag. It was on this spot on 17 February 1933 that the Nazis took control of German government by burning down the Reichstag building and then blaming the fire on the Communist Party. Russian soldiers were so determined to have their revenge in 1945 that they ignored direct commands in order to achieve the honour of being the first company to hoist the Russian flag over the Reichstag dome. You can still see the graffiti marks made in the foyer by the conquering Soviets. The recent contribution of an inspiring glass dome designed by Sir Norman Foster brings the building into the 21st century and is a fitting structure to mark the return of government to the German capital. (*See pp. 18, 62.*)

SAMMLUNG DAIMLERCHRYSLER

🛈 Alte Potsdamer Strasse 5

📞 2594 1420

www.sammlung.daimlerchrysler.com

☀ 11:00am–7:00pm daily

Ⓜ U-Bahn/S-Bahn Potsdamer Platz Free

A corporate contribution to Berlin's already influential modern art scene, Sammlung Daimler-Chrysler concentrates on 20th-century abstract and conceptual art. Sometimes stimulating, other times a load of art wank – the decision is yours. Jeff Koons and Andy Warhol are just two of the big names you might be familiar with. Architects take note: this is the only original house left on Potsdamer Platz after the recent construction boom.

SIEGESSÄULE

🛈 Strasse des 17 Juni

☎ 391 2961

🕓 Summer, Mon 9:30am–6:30pm; Tues–Thurs, Fri 9:30am–7:00pm; Sat 9:30am–8:00pm; Winter, Mon 9:30am–5:30pm; Tues–Sat 9:30am–6:00pm

Ⓤ S-Bahn Bellevue

💰 €1.20. No credit cards

One of the best views in Berlin, Siegessäule is Berlin's tallest monument. Built in 1871-3,

the column commemorates Prussian military success against Denmark, Austria and France. A gilded Goddess of Victoria stands at the top surrounded by captured French cannons and cannon-balls. A climb up the 285-step spiral staircase provides a wonderful panorama of Tiergarten.

Marlene Dietrich

Falling in love again – that's what Berliners are finally doing when it comes to the memory of its most famous film export, Marlene Dietrich. Born just over 100 years ago in the German capital (her 100th birthday was celebrated in 2001 with a square named in her honour), Ms. Dietrich shot to fame in the German film industry of the 1930s, specifically in the masterpieces directed by Josef Von Sternberg. Hollywood sat up and took notice of her striking good looks and riveting talent in 1930 with the release of *Der Blaue Engel* (*The Blue Angel*) in which she plays femme fatale nightclub singer Lola. This is where her famed top hat, tails and fishnet stockings look made its appearance, a look that stayed with her almost until her death.

A popular fixture on the gay scene of the 1920s, Dietrich spent much of her time hanging out with queer artists and happy homosexuals in the swinging bars off Nollendorfplatz. Although she was married to Czech production assistant Rudolf Sieber and had one daughter with him, Maria Riva, rumours circulated for many years that Marlene was actually a Sapphic sister.

Ms. Dietrich hasn't always been one of Berlin's most treasured performers – her decision to leave Berlin following the rise of the Nazi party left many locals feeling that she had abandoned Germany and turned her back on her roots. Desperate to keep her career going in an America with a strong distaste for anything Germanic, Marlene became one of the army's most powerful weapons, performing an almost non stop schedule of concerts and stage shows for the U.S.O. But, she never recaptured the adoration of her home country during her lifetime and never felt she could return to the city she loved most. Exiling herself to Paris in her golden years, Marlene avoided Berlin as much as she possibly could. It wasn't until her death in 1992 that her wish to return came true. She is now buried in Friedhof Friedenau cemetery on Fehlerstrasse in Schöneberg.

For a crash–course in Dietrich film, be sure to watch *Morocco* (1930), *Dishonoured* (1931), *Shanghai Express* and *Blonde Venus* (1932), *The Scarlet Empress* (1934) and *The Devil is a Woman* (1935), in addition to the previously mentioned *Blue Angel* (1930).

All Shopped Out

Shopping will never be Berlin's strongest selling point. This is the land where the mullet is considered *en vogue*, remember? Go to Paris, London or New York if top togs are your idea of a perfect vacation. Come to Berlin if secret finds are more what you had in mind. Everything from Art Deco gems to GDR soldier outfits can be found if you look hard enough. You may not wind up looking like a supermodel, but the items you bring back will be sure to be treasured a lot more than a shirt that goes out of fashion in a year.

Top of the Shops

Coration

ℹ️ Kastanienallee 13, Prenzlauer Berg 📞 4404 6090 ☀️ Mon–Tues 2:00pm–8:00pm; Wed–Fri 12:00pm–8:00pm; Sat 11:00am–6:00pm 🚇 U-Bahn Eberswalder Strasse 💳 V, MC, AmEx

Dot.com millionaires, geeky science types and urban hipsters love the minimalist clothes on offer at this trendy German boutique popular amongst the fickle Prenzlauer Berg set. Black and its various shades tend to be the order of the day so colour freaks are advised to steer clear. A good resource for cocktail drinkers and business dealings. Not so much for the club-kid in all of us.

Harvey's

ℹ️ Kurfürstendamm 186, Charlottenburg 📞 883 3803 ☀️ Mon–Fri 10:30am–8:30pm; Sat 10:00am–4:00pm 🚇 U-Bahn Uhlandstrasse 💳 V, MC, AmEx

Cutting edge men's fashion with a strong focus on Japanese (Yamamoto, Comme des Garçons) and Belgian (Bikkembergs) designers. Prices aren't outrageous considering what's on offer, but you'll still need a second mortgage to afford even a small bow–tie in this place. Shopping here can get slightly claustrophobic and difficult. The place is stocked to the rafters with goods and everything is wrapped in its original plastic and folded tightly on shelves, making it difficult to browse. Good, especially during sale seasons.

KaDeWe

🛈 Tauentzienstrasse
21–4, Schöneberg
📞 21210   🕑 Mon–Fri
9:30am–8:00pm; Sat
9:00am–4:00pm
🚇 U-Bahn
Wittenbergplatz
💳 V, MC, AmEx, DC

The only department store you'll ever need in Berlin, this is the city's Harrods, complete with a glorious food hall on the fifth floor. A good place to buy basics, including underwear, luggage and toiletries; the clothing departments are a bit underwhelming. Not exactly the place to go if you need to make a statement without saying a word. Ladies have a bit more luck than

gentlemen, with a few hidden treasures available on floors three and four. (*See p.26.*)

Mientus Studio 2002

🛈 Wilmersdorfer Strasse 73, Charlottenburg
📞 323 9077   🕑 Mon–Fri 10:00am–8:30pm; Sat
10:00am–4:00pm   💳 V, MC, AmEx, DC

Conservative with a capital C, Mientus Studio 2002 caters to a more genteel Charlottenburg crowd with its selection of Joop!, Miu Miu and Boss merchandise. Bankers, financiers and capitalist types come here for the well-cut suits, hushed service and dependable classics. Outrageous is definitely not the key–word here. And no matter what the designers say, black and navy will always be the in-season colours at this shopping Mecca.

Mondos Arts

🛈 Schreinerstrasse 6, Friedrichshain
📞 4201 778   www.mondosarts.de
🕑 Mon–Fri 10:00am–7:00pm; Sat 11:00am–4:00pm
🚇 U-Bahn Samariter Strasse
💳 V, MC, AmEx

German souvenirs with a twist – this antiques find stocks only merchandise related to or directly from the East German Cold War period. Propaganda posters, Soviet flags, army fatigues and pounding East German rock CDs make for unique reminders of your visit. My favourite items are anything featuring the Ampelmännchen figure found on street signals throughout East Berlin. He's the peasant figure with the delightful hat you'll see flashing your way across avenues in Mitte, Prenz'l Berg and Friedrichshain.

A bit of luxe

Planet

ℹ️ Schlüterstrasse 35, Charlottenburg 📞 885 2717 🕐 Mon–Fri 11:00am–8:00pm; Sat 11:00am–4:00pm Ⓥ U-Bahn Uhlandstrasse V, MC, AmEx

Going clubbing but haven't got a thing to wear? Planet specialises in solving your disco crisis with its array of lamé, leather and latex wear, perfect for any outrageous occasion. A bit "two years ago" with its offerings, the clothes are more flash and dazzle as opposed to the cutting-edge chic you might find in other metropolises. Custom-designed leather accessories are a specialty and worth every penny if you have the time to wait while they're created for you.

Prinz Eisenherz

ℹ️ Bleibtreustrasse 52, Charlottenburg 📞 313 9936 www.prinz-eisenherz.com
🕐 Mon–Fri 10:00am–6:00pm; Sat 10:00am–4:00pm 🚇 S-Bahn Savignyplatz Ⓥ V, MC

Berlin's best queer bookstore, Prinz Eisenherz has a large selection of gay, lesbian and trans literature on hand in both English and German. Signings and special events are often held in-store and the front window is a great resource centre for those looking for more information on perfectly pink happenings in and around town. A small porn section is in the rear of the shop, but it doesn't constitute the bulk of the stock.

Quartier 206

ℹ️ Friedrichstrasse 71, Mitte 📞 2094 6800
🕐 Mon–Fri 10:00am–8:00pm; Sat; 10:00am–4:00pm
🚇 U-Bahn Stadtmitte
Ⓥ V, MC, AmEx, DC

A department store with a difference – Quartier 206 is the shop that upped Mitte in the style stakes with its selection of cutting-edge designer

Stairway to shopping heaven

togs. Everything from Prada to Paul Smith, Dries Van Noten to Dolce is on offer, and that's not including the vast women's section with its array of pricey and passionate clothing and accessories. Neither wildly unwearable nor boringly staid, the clothes are well purchased by the team of in-store buyers and cater to shoppers who know their stuff. Staff are genuinely friendly and lack the pretentiousness often found in stores of the same calibre. (See p.41.)

Schwarze Mode

ℹ Grunewaldstrasse 91, Schöneberg
☎ 784 5922 🕐 Mon–Fri
12:00pm–7:00pm; Sat 10:00am–4:00pm
Ⓜ U-Bahn Kleistpark 💳 V, MC, AmEx,
DC

Leathers and latex and rubber –
oh my! Berlin is the undisputed
capital of European fetish, and
Schwarze Mode offers it all.
From dildos to butt plugs,
restraints to chaps – if it's made
out of rubber or cowhide, then
they'll have it here. And if they
don't, then they'll custom-make
whatever you're looking for.
Schwarze Mode is welcoming
to both men and women,
making it one of the better
options for leather-loving
lesbians in this town's traditionally male-focused SM scene.

Stilwerk

ℹ Kantstrasse 17, Charlottenburg 315
150 🕐 Mon–Fri 10:00am–8:00pm; Sat
10:00am–4:00pm; Viewing only, Sun
2:00pm–6:00pm Ⓜ S-Bahn Savignyplatz
💳 V, MC, AmEx, DC

If you love IKEA but are looking
for something with a bit of
originality then Stilwerk may have
just what you're looking for. Home
furnishings, lighting fixtures,
interiors and kitchenware are
jumbled into one massive and
convenient location – and all
feature the European flair that 20
and 30-something homeowners are
flocking to furnish with. A bit
more upscale than the popular
Swedish label, prices reflect this
upmarket sensibility. Lighting is
one of their better departments,
but check currents and plugs.

Home shopping at Stilwerk

Shop Around

ANTIQUES

DECO ARTS

Motzstrasse 6, Schöneberg 215 8672 Wed–Fri 3:00pm–6:30pm; Sat 11:00am–3:00pm U-Bahn Nollendorfplatz No credit cards.

For that Sally Bowles touch, Deco Arts is the place to go. 30s furniture and décor is the focus, making it a great place to transform your home into a set–piece from the film *Metropolis*.

RADIO ART

Zossener Strasse 2, Kreuzberg 693 9435 Thurs–Fri 12:00pm–6:00pm; Sat 10:00am–1:00pm U-Bahn Gneisenaustrasse V, MC, AmEx

Antique radios are the only thing on offer at this quirky shop. It may sound boring but they're actually a lot more interesting than you might think. Note the strange opening hours to avoid disappointment.

BOOKS

BOOKS IN BERLIN

Goethestrasse 69, Charlottenburg 313 1233 Mon–Fri 12:00pm–8:00pm; Sat 10:00am–4:00pm S-Bahn Savignyplatz V

Berlin's largest resource for English-language books. Everything from fiction to fact is available, including the usual bestsellers and classic novels. Don't go looking for anything too obscure. Special orders can be done for rarities and hard-to-finds.

CLUBWEAR

GROOPIE DELUXE

Goltzstrasse 39, Schöneberg 217 2038 Mon–Fri 11:00am–7:00pm; Sat 11:00am–4:00pm U-Bahn Eisenacher Strasse V, MC, AmEx

Frills, fake fur, feather boas – if you want fun fashion then this is the place to come. Outfits for both men and women are available. Only for the truly daring.

TENDERLOIN

Alte Schönhauser Strasse 30, Mitte 4201 5785 Mon–Fri 12:00pm–8:00pm; Sat 12:00pm–4:00pm U-Bahn Weinmeisterstrasse V, MC, AmEx

Styles and stock change almost daily at

Radio days

this retro shop with a thing for all things now. One day it could be Pucci prints, the next, a salute to Edwardian velvet. A special place for a one-off original.

DEPARTMENT STORES

GALERIES LAFAYETTE
ⓘ Französische Strasse 23, Mitte 🔗 209 480 ☀ Mon-Sat 10:00am–10:00pm
🚇 U-Bahn/S-Bahn Friedrichstrasse
💳 V, MC, AmEx

The Berlin branch of the famed Parisian department store. Stock is nothing to go gaga over, but the glass dome in the lobby is truly inspiring.
(See p.41.)

DESIGNER

CHITON
ⓘ Goltzstrasse 12, Schöneberg 🔗 216 6013 ☀ Mon-Fri 12:00pm–6:30pm; Sat 11:00am–2:00pm
🚇 U-Bahn Eisenacher Strasse 💳 V, MC, AmEx

The best made-to-measure place in town for original suits and dresses. Minimalist is the key word here – albeit minimalist done very, very well. Allow two to three weeks for a dress or a custom made suit.

CLAUDIA SKODA LEVEL
ⓘ Linienstrasse 156, Mitte 🔗 280 7211 ☀ Mon–Fri 11:00am– 7:00pm
🚇 U-Bahn Oranienburger Tor 💳 V, MC, AmEx, DC

Modern fabrics and

funky knitwear for the adventurous lady or gentleman. No virgin wool jumpers here, thank you very much. Body-conscious togs are what's on offer, so if you haven't been to the gym in a while, don't bother shopping here.

JIL SANDER
ⓘ Kurfürstendamm 185, Charlottenburg
🔗 886 7020
☀ Mon–Fri 10:00am– 7:00pm; Sat 10:00am– 4:00pm 🚇 U-Bahn Kurfürstendamm
💳 V, MC, AmEx

Germany's biggest contribution to the world of haute couture may now be owned by Prada, but that doesn't stop the label from being one of the most popular in the country. Sleek, chic, black and modern are the elements of Jil Sander design. Expensive and outrageous are the elements of a JilSander price tag.

MOLOTOW
ⓘ Gneisenaustrasse 112, Kreuzberg 🔗 693 0818 ☀ Mon–Fri 2:00pm– 8:00pm; Sat 12:00pm– 4:00pm 🚇 U-Bahn Mehringdamm
💳 V, MC, AmEx, DC

Yes, there are clothes at Molotow, but locals

Through the looking glass

swear by this shop for
their selection of hats.
So if you need a topper
for your favourite top
then this is the place to
pick one up.

PATRICK HELLMAN
ℹ️ Fasanenstrasse 26,
Charlottenburg
📞 8848 7712
⏰ Mon–Wed, Fri
10:00am–7:00pm; Thurs
10:00am–8:00pm; Sat
10:00am–4:00pm
🚇 U-Bahn Uhlandstrasse
💳 V, MC, AmEx, DC

Italian design for men
is Patrick Hellman's
speciality. Sharp suiting
and casual cashmeres
deck out the yachting

set in outfits from the
likes of Zegna and Pal
Zileri. Bespoke
tailoring is also available.

RESPECTMEN
ℹ️ Neue Schönhauser
Strasse 14, Mitte
📞 283 5010 ⏰ Mon–Fri
12:00pm–8:00pm; Sat
11:00am–4:00pm 🚇 U-
Bahn Weinmeister-strasse
💳 V, MC, AmEx

I love RespectMen for
their selection of both
conservative and trendy
clothes that will outfit
you for every event
from a business lunch
to a night on the town.
RespectWomen and
RespectLess are located

a few steps further
down the same street.

TOOLS & GALLERY
ℹ️ Rosenthaler Strasse
34–5, Mitte 📞 2859 9343
⏰ Mon–Fri 10:00am–
8:00pm; Sat 10:00am–
4:00pm
🚇 S-Bahn Hackescher
Markt 💳 V, MC

Westwood, McQueen
… if it's hot then Tools
& Gallery will have it.
Too bad the staff are so
pretentious, making
any jaunt inside
distasteful. Avoid if you
can – even if their
stock contains some
of the most stunning
pieces in town.

Something for the weekend

FETISH

BLACK STYLE

🛈 Seelower Strasse 5, Prenzlauer Berg

✆ 4468 8595

www.blackstyle.de

☀ Mon–Wed, Fri 1:00pm–6:30pm; Thurs 1:00pm–8:00pm; Sat 10:00am–2:00pm Ⓤ U-Bahn/S-Bahn Schönhauser Allee

💳 V, MC, AmEx

Rubber and latex fetish gear for the gummi in you. Prices are good and mail order is available.

MISTER B

🛈 Nollendorfstrasse 23, Schöneberg ✆ 2199 7704 www.misterb.com

☀ Mon–Fri 12:00pm–8:00pm; Sat 11:00am–4:00pm Ⓤ U-Bahn Nollendorfplatz 💳 V, MC

With branches in London and Amsterdam, Mr. B could be considered the Gap of the fetish world. Hardcore enthusiasts will swear blind that this is the best fetish shop in town. Women may not agree – the place isn't exactly friendly to ladies.

LEATHERS

🛈 Schliemannstrasse 38, Prenzlauer Berg

✆ 442 7786

www.leathers-berlin.de

☀ Tues-Fri 12:00pm–7:30pm; Sat 12:00pm–4:00pm Ⓤ U-Bahn Eberswalder Strasse

💳 V, MC, AmEx

Another leather shop with friendly staff and tons of SM stuff to choose from. A selection of fetish furniture is what makes this shop unique.

LUGGAGE

BREE

🛈 Kurfürstendamm 44, Charlottenburg

✆ 883 7462 ☀ Mon–Fri 10:00am–7:00pm; Sat 10:00am–4:00pm

🅤 U-Bahn Uhlandstrasse
🅥 V, MC, AmEx

High-quality German luggage for those of you who want quality without little LV's scattered all over your suitcases. Purses, wallets and carryalls are also on the menu.

MUSIC

GELBE MUSIK
ℹ️ Schaperstrasse 11, Wilmersdorf 📞 211 3962
⏰ Tues–Fri 1:00pm–6:00pm; Sat 11:00am–2:00pm
🅤 U-Bahn Augsburger Strasse 🅥 V, MC

Avant-garde, minimalist, electronic, industrial. If it bleeps and it's rare, then they'll have it here.

MR DEAD & MRS FREE
ℹ️ Bülowstrasse 5, Schöneberg 📞 215 1449
⏰ Mon–Wed 11:00am–7:00pm; Thurs–Fri 11:00am–8:00pm; Sat 11:00am–4:00pm
🅤 U-Bahn Nollendorfplatz
🅥 V

Second-hand and rare CDs at bargain prices. Mr Dead & Mrs Free carries just about everything, but there is a slight slant towards

artists who have found Berlin to inspire them, including Bowie and Nick Cave.

SOUVENIRS

J & M FÄSSLER
ℹ️ Europa-Center, Charlottenburg
📞 342 7166
⏰ 10:00am–6:30pm Mon–Fri, 10:00am–6:00pm Sat
🅤 U-Bahn/S-Bahn Zoologischer Garten
🅥 V, MC, AmEx, DC

Nasty beer steins, yodelling bears, cuckoo clocks, collectible spoons – yippee!

Treats and toys

Modern Art

Berlin has always been at the cutting edge of something. Whether it be film and sexual politics in the 20s and 30s or techno music and underground house in the 80s, Berlin's scenesters have always had an eye for the outrageous and the inspiring. David Bowie certainly thought so when he uprooted himself from London to follow his musical passions to Berlin. The bisexual king of glam rock moved to the German capital in 1976 to experience the artistic buzz of the walled city, moving into the same house as Iggy Pop. In the 1980s it was Australian Nick Cave and Depeche Mode's Martin Gore who flocked to the blossoming electronic scene in search of a more industrial and gritty sound. You can still see the home of Bowie and Pop in Schöneberg on Hauptstrasse. Bowie had a spacious first-floor abode while Iggy has a cramped studio in the rear Hinterhof.

Artistic expression has always been one of the prime motivating forces for Berlin residents. Experimentation began in the early 20th century with the avant-garde work of Brecht, Reinhardt, Weill and Schönberg. From theatre to music and now to art, Berlin's tastes in experimentation have led it to drop its mantle as theatre capital or rocking music town in favour of the world of conceptualism and post-modernism. Young, contemporary artists consider Berlin to be the supreme city in which to make their breakthrough. Enigmatic, ever-changing, but wonderful once you get a handle on it, the German capital can make or break new talent.

Today, if you want to add a little art to your life, Mitte is the best place to find top-quality pieces. By the time this book is printed, however, that statement could be completely false. The gallery scene in Berlin changes frequently depending upon rent costs, gallery popularity and neighbourhood trends. One of the safer bets for a look at what's hot, fresh and new is

Accessible art

he collection of spaces on Holzmarktstrasse. Art Mile
(Auguststrasse), while losing popularity, is another option
or interested buyers.

OWIE'S HOME

ⓘ Hauptstrasse 152, Schöneberg

☎ No phone.

⏰ 24hrs daily (It's a residential home)

Ⓜ U-Bahn Kleistpark

Ⓕ Free

ÜRO FRIEDRICH

ⓘ Holzmarktstrasse 15–18, Mitte

☎ 2016 5115

ww.buerofriedrich.org

⏰ Tues–Fri 1:00pm-7:00pm; Sat–Sun
00pm–6:00pm

Ⓜ U-Bahn/S-Bahn Jannowitzbrücke

Ⓝ No credit cards

CARLIER/GEBAUER

ⓘ Holzmarktstrasse 15–18, Mitte

☎ 280 8110

www.carliergebauer.com

⏰ Tues–Sat 12:00pm–6:00pm

Ⓜ U-Bahn/S-Bahn Jannowitzbrücke

Ⓥ V

CHOUAKRI BRAHMS BERLIN

ⓘ Holzmarktstrasse 15–18, Mitte

☎ 2839 1153

www.chouakri-brahms-berlin.com

⏰ Tues–Sat 11:00am–6:00pm

Ⓜ U-Bahn/S-Bahn Jannowitzbrücke

Ⓝ No credit cards

Eating Out

Berlin has come a long way from the days when a bratwurst and a pretzel were considered haute cuisine. Waves of Asian and Middle Eastern immigration and a long period of American forces occupation helped change all of that. Chefs are abandoning the standard pork leg and two veg dishes of yesteryear in favour of delicately spiced fusion dishes. All the better for your picky palate, is what I say. Select from the recommendations on the next few pages to make your trip a feast for the taste buds.

Cream of the Cuisine

Abendmahl

ℹ️ Muskauer Strasse 9, Kreuzberg 📞 612 5170 🕑 6:00pm–1:00am daily.
🚇 U-Bahn Görlitzer Bahnhof 🥗 🍽️ No credit cards

In a city where sausage is king, Abendmahl makes for a nice change. The primo vegetarian restaurant in town, you won't see a speck of speck on the menu. Reservations are highly recommended as the quality of their cuisine isn't a hidden secret. And if your date happens to want something with a pulse, you'll be pleased to know that fish dishes are available.

Adlon

ℹ️ Unter den Linden 77, Mitte 📞 2261 1555
🕑 Tues–Sat 6:00pm–11:00pm 🚉 S-Bahn Unter den Linden 🥗 🍽️ V, AmEx, DC

The following price guides have been used for eating out and indicate the price for a main course:

🍽️ = cheap = under €8

🍽️ = moderate = €8–€22

🍽️ = expensive = €22 +

EATING OUT

The fanciest hotel in town can boast one of the fanciest eateries in Mitte. The Adlon, in addition to having some of the finest views of the Brandenburg Gate and Unter den Linden after dark, also has a wonderful dining room serving up dishes of international fusion cuisine. Booking is essential. Perfect for that intimate dinner for two or any special occasion.

Time for a French snack

Art

ℹ️ Fasanenstrasse 81A, Charlottenburg 📞 313 2625 www.art-restaurant.com ⏰ Mon–Fri 12:00pm–2:00am; Sat–Sun 10:30am–2:00am 🚇 U-Bahn/S-Bahn Zoologischer Garten 🐱 💳 – 💳 No credit cards

Food isn't the main course on offer at Art. It's a big gay hotspot with exposed brick walls and a fine outdoor patio for al-fresco dining on warm summer days. It can get a little noisy sometimes due to its location directly under the U-Bahn tracks, but you'll hardly notice it over the din of the music and the clinking of glasses. Pastas, sandwiches and salads constitute the bulk of what's on offer.

Austria

ℹ️ Bergmannstrasse 30, Kreuzberg 📞 694 4440 ⏰ Sept–May 6:00pm–1:00am daily; June–Aug 7:00pm–1:00am daily. 🚇 U-Bahn Gneisenaustrasse 🐱 💳 V, MC

For a taste of old oom-pah-pah, drag your lederhosen down to Austria. Resembling a German hunting lodge inside – complete with deer antlers and wooden-beamed ceilings, Austria dishes up hearty Germanic food with a strong focus on meat, meat and more meat. Everything is organic, so you won't have to worry about the European problem of BSE. For a true treat, I recommend the overwhelmingly excellent Schnitzel.

Café Berio

ℹ️ Maassenstrasse 7, Schöneberg 📞 216 1946 www.berio.de ⏰ 8:00am–1:00am daily. 🚇 U-Bahn Nollendorfplatz 🐱 💳 No credit cards

Café Berio is more scene than suppertime location. Excellent coffees and pastries have made this place a gay hotspot with excellent people-watching just off Nollendorfplatz. Reasonably priced sandwiches are available should you want something a little more substantial, but most who go here are usually looking for something a bit more solid to put into their mouths – and I don't mean food. Not a place to go to if you're looking to crash out in your trackies and a ratty T-shirt.

Fleischerei Bachhuber's bei Witty's

ⓘ Wittenbergplatz, Charlottenburg. 📞 No phone. 🕒 11:00am–1:00am daily
Ⓜ U-Bahn Wittenbergplatz 💳 🍴 No credit cards

Fritz & Co. may have the gay community's support in the
Wittenbergplatz wurst stakes, but when it comes to quality, Witty's is
hard to beat. Conveniently located directly outside the entrance to
KaDeWe, the menu contains your standard sausage offerings and chip
possibilities. For my money, this is the best place to grab a dog in West
Berlin, primarily due to its organic-only meat policy and ice-cold
drinks. For some reason, frozen chunks of water are a rarity in this town.

Kellerrestaurant im Brecht-Haus

ⓘ Chausseestrasse 125, Mitte 📞 282 3843
🕒 Summer, Mon–Fri 12:00pm–1:00am; Sun 6:00pm–1:00am; Winter 6:00pm–1:00am
daily. Ⓜ U-Bahn Oranienburger Tor 💳 🍴 V, MC, AmEx

For home-cooked dinner (well Bertolt Brecht's home, that is) take a
cultural trip to the Kellerrestaurant im Brecht-Haus. Everything available
is derived from Brecht's favourite dishes, originally prepared by his
partner Helene Weigel. Crammed full of old stage memorabilia and
Brecht treasures, dining here is a theatrical buff's paradise.

Comfort at Adlon

EATING OUT

Lukiluki

ℹ️ Motzstrasse 28, Schöneberg
🌀 2362 2079
www.lukiluki.de
🕕 6:00pm–2:00am daily. 🚇 U-Bahn Nollendorfplatz
💳 🍽️ No credit cards

A taste of Thailand

There's not much to recommend this gay favourite. The Thai food is merely passable and the service can be rather slow. So why is the place packed almost every night? Three reasons. Its location is unbeatable if you're planning a long night out in Schöneberg; it's open until the wee hours of the morning; and every buff male waiter on staff works topless. Go for the eye candy but don't expect much from the limited menu.

Sabu

ℹ️ Pfalzburger Strasse 20, Charlottenburg
🌀 8639 4173
www.sabu-ro.de
🕕 Tues–Sun 5:00pm–midnight
🚇 U-Bahn Hohenzollernplatz
💳 🍽️ MC

Considered the finest Japanese restaurant in Berlin, Sabu boasts almost 20 years' experience serving sushi, tempura and teriyaki to the starving masses. Lunches are especially good if you're on the go. The darling bento boxes are packed with goodies you can take on the run. It's a hell of a better option than wolfing down a Number 3 combo from McDonald's.

Woolloomooloo

ℹ️ Rontgenstrasse 7, Charlottenburg
🌀 3470 2777 🕕 5:00pm–1:00am daily.
🚇 U-Bahn Richard-Wagner-Platz
💳 🍽️ V, MC

Antipodeans will feel like they're back down under at Woolloomooloo. Ostrich, kangaroo, crocodile – it's all available here at one of Berlin's only Pacific Rim speciality restaurants. Germans find this place a tad quirky due to its copious use of exotic spices and coconut milk. You'll find it tasty and top-notch. It's also one of the only dining spots to offer Australian vineyard options on the wine list.

Charlottenburg & Wilmersdorf

FLORIAN

🛈 Grolmanstrasse 52

📞 313 9184

🕐 6:00pm–3:00am daily.

🚇 S-Bahn Savignyplatz

💳 📋

No credit cards

South German food popular with media types, theatricals and the film industry. Good staff and selection make the place perpetually full.

HEINRICH

🛈 Sophie-Charlotten-Strasse 88 📞 321 6517

🕐 4:00pm–midnight daily.

🚇 U-Bahn Sophie-Charlotten-Platz

💳 📋

V, MC, AmEx

German dishes and a wide range of vegetarian options for those who want native cuisine with a bit of a twist. Ever wanted to try horse ragout? Then try it here.

JIMMY'S DINER

🛈 Pariser Strasse 41

📞 886 0607

🕐 Sun–Thurs 12:00pm–2:00am; Fri-Sat 12:00pm–4:00am 🚇 U-Bahn Hohenzollernplatz

💳 📋

No credit cards

Missing home? Drop by Jimmy's for a great selection of American meals. The hamburgers are especially huge and tasty. A good place to mix with the expat community who frequent the place.

MARJELLCHEN

🛈 Mommsenstrasse 9

📞 883 2676

🕐 Mon–Sat 5:00pm–midnight 🚇 S-Bahn Savignyplatz 💳 📋

V, MC, AmEx, DC

Specialities from East Prussia, Pomerania and Silesia. Russia may control its borders, but nothing will ever control the owner's frequent penchant to break out into song.

MESA

🛈 Paretzer Strasse 5

📞 822 5364

🕐 4:00pm–midnight daily.

🚇 U-Bahn Heidelberger Platz 💳 📋 V, AmEx

Lebanese tucker, including couscous, lamb dishes galore and vegetable rösti.

PARIS BAR

🛈 Kantstrasse 152

📞 313 8052

🕐 12:00pm–2:00am daily.

🚇 S-Bahn Savignyplatz

💳 📋 V, MC, AmEx

French food in an atmosphere that feels like you just stepped off the Champs-

Best of the Rest

Elysées. Art drips from every corner and you fully expect the cast of the Moulin Rouge to walk in at any moment.

SACHIKO SUSHI

ℹ️ Grolmanstrasse 47
📞 313 2282 ⏰ 12:00pm–midnight daily 🚇 S-Bahn Savignyplatz 👕 🍴 No credit cards

Berlin's only sushi bar with a revolving trolley, all of the dishes on offer are absolutely scrumptious. Choose your selections by picking the plates off the whirling boats and adding the number of morsels you eat to your running tab.

Kreuzberg & Schöneberg

ALTES ZOLLHAUS

ℹ️ Carl-Herz-Ufer 30
📞 692 3300
⏰ Tues–Sat 6:00pm–11:30pm
🚇 U-Bahn Prinzenstrasse
👕 🍴 full menu V, MC, AmEx, DC

German dishes in a quiet, riverside inn. Portion sizes are bigger than the norm and all ingredients come from Brandenburg's organic farms.

CAFÉ EINSTEIN

ℹ️ 58 Kurfürstenstrasse
📞 261 5096
⏰ 9:00am–2:00am daily.

🚇 U-Bahn Kurfürstenstrasse
👕 🍴 V, AmEx, DC

Old Vienna comes to Berlin in this atmospheric coffee shop dedicated to Austrian num-nums. The apple strudel is absolutely amazing and the coffee is ten times better than any Starbucks.

CAFÉ POSITHIV

ℹ️ Alvenslebenstrasse 26
📞 216 8654 ⏰ Tues–Fri 3:00pm–11:00pm; Sat 6:00pm–late (posted hours may not always be adhered to) 🚇 U-Bahn Bülowstrasse
👕 🍴 No credit cards

Sandwiches and light snacks at this volunteer-run café. All monies earned by the place go towards supporting local gay charities.

ÇARDAK

ℹ️ Isenacher Strasse 54
📞 782 7172
⏰ Tues–Thurs 12:00pm–midnight; Fri–Sat 4:00pm–3:00am; Sun 10:00am–midnight
🚇 U-Bahn Eisenacher Strasse 👕 🚇 – 🍴
 No credit cards

Fine Turkish cuisine popular with hip 20-something Turks. Live music and divan-based dining available on weekends. A perfect

place to warm your bones with a spicy soup on a cold winter night.

CHANDRA KUMARI

ℹ️ Gneisenaustrasse 4
📞 694 3056 ⏰ 12:00pm–1:00am daily. 🚇 U-Bahn Mehringdamm 👕 🍴
No credit cards

Eye-watering curries and spicy vegetables at Berlin's only Sri Lankan restaurant. Milkshakes and exotic fruits complete the tasty package.

HABIBI

ℹ️ Goltzstrasse 24
📞 215 3332 ⏰ Mon-Fri Sun 11:00am–3:00am; Sat 11:00am–5:00am 🚇 U-Bahn Nollendorfplatz
👕 🍴 No credit cards.

Fresh Middle Eastern dishes, including falafel, tabouli, grilled aubergine and freshly squeezed juices. Good for a quick yet tasty bite.

HAKUIN

ℹ️ Martin-Luther-Strasse 1
📞 218 2027 ⏰ Tues–Sat 5:00pm–11:30pm; Sun 12:00pm–11:30pm
🚇 U-Bahn Wittenbergplatz
👕 🍴 V, MC, DC

Buddhist vegetarian food in an exotic, jungle-like atmosphere. The fruit-based curries come highly recommended.

HASIR

ℹ️ Adalbertstrasse 10
📞 614 2372
🌐 www.hasir.de
24hrs daily. Ⓤ U-Bahn
Kottbusser Tor 🃏 🎖️
No credit cards

Every backpacker and drunkard knows that the doner kebab is the refuge of the poor and inebriated. This is the place that created the things back in 1971. Thought they were authentically Turkish? Think again. Come worship at the temple that launched a thousand puddles of vomit around the world.

HENNE

ℹ️ Leuschnerdamm 25
📞 614 7730
🌐 Tues–Sun 7:00pm–1:00am Ⓤ U-Bahn
Kottbusser Tor
🃏 🎖️
No credit cards

Henne serves four things. Half a roast chicken, potato salad, cabbage and beer. The chicken comes with either the cabbage or the potato salad depending on what you choose. Limited menu options but fabulous results.

INDIA HAUS

ℹ️ Feuringstrasse 38
📞 781 2546

🌐 Mon–Fri 5:00pm–midnight; Sat–Sun 12:00pm–1:00am
Ⓤ U-Bahn/S-Bahn Innsbrucker Platz
🃏 🎖️ V, AmEx, DC

Unlike London, Berlin is limited when it comes to Indian food. This is one of the better options, with a typical menu of kormas, tikka masalas and tandooris.

LA COCOTTE

ℹ️ Vorbergstrasse 10
📞 7895 7658 🌐 6:00pm–1:00am daily Ⓤ U-Bahn
Eisenacher Strasse
🃏 🎖️ – 🃏 🎖️ V, MC

French cuisine popular with the gay community. Food isn't spectacular but the scenery and dating options are.

MARKTHALLE

ℹ️ Pücklerstrasse 34

📞 617 5502
🌐 Mon–Thurs 9:00am–2:00am; Fri–Sat 8:00am–4:00am; Sun 10:00am–2:00pm Ⓤ U-Bahn
Görlitzer Bahnhof 🃏 🎖️
V, MC, AmEx

A Kreuzberg institution famous for its weekend breakfasts served until 5:00pm. Late-night clubkids call this German restaurant home-away-from-home.

OMNES

ℹ️ Motzstrasse 8
📞 2363 8300
www.cafe-omnes.de
🌐 24hrs daily. Meals only from 4:00pm–midnight.
Ⓤ U-Bahn Nollendorfplatz
🃏 🎖️ No credit cards.

A popular gay eatery and lounge for reasons I'm still trying to figure out. Dead during the week, things hot up on weekends and in the

Great coffee and strudel at Café Einstein

summer when the vast front window is opened up to allow better vantages for a quick pickup. Light snacks served.

OSTERIA NO 1

ⓘ Kreuzbergstrasse 71 ⓐ 786 9162 ⏰ 12:00pm–1:00am daily ⓜ U-Bahn Mehringdamm ⓥ ⓒ V, MC, AmEx, DC

The best Italian restaurant in town run by a family of famed restaurateurs. The three-course lunch menu is a particularly good deal.

PAGODA

ⓘ Bergmannstrasse 88 ⓐ 691 2640 ⏰ 12:00pm–midnight daily ⓜ U-Bahn Gneisenaustrasse ⓥ ⓒ
No credit cards

Authentic Thai food prepared right in front

of you. Always packed, extra seating is available downstairs if you think it's too full.

MITTE

CAFÉ OREN

ⓘ Oranienburger Strasse 28 ⓐ 282 8228 ⏰ Mon–Fri 12:00pm–1:00am; Sat– Sun 10:00am–1:00am ⓜ S-Bahn Oranienburger Strasse ⓥ ⓒ V, AmEx

Locals call this place a Jewish restaurant but it's actually more Middle Eastern in tone. *Falafel, tabouli* and *humus* litter the menu tastily. Please note that the restaurant is not kosher.

GANYMED

ⓘ Schiffbauerdamm 5 ⓐ 2859 9046 ⏰ Summer Mon–Fri 11:30am–1:00am; Sat

10:00am–1:00am; Winter Mon–Sat 6:00pm–1:00am; Sun 11:30am–1:00am ⓜ U-Bahn/S-Bahn Friedrichstrasse ⓥ ⓒ V, MC, AmEx, DC

Once the GDR's most exclusive restaurant, Ganymed has a bit of a 'throwback to the old Soviet era' feel to it. A great place to come if you're going to a show at the Berliner Ensemble or if you're a wine connoisseur. Ganymed has the best cellar in town.

GUY

ⓘ Jägerstrasse 59–60 ⓐ 2094 2600 ⏰ Mon–Fri 12:00pm–3:00pm, 6:00pm –1:00am; Sat 6:00pm–1:00am ⓜ U-Bahn Französische Strasse ⓥ ⓒ V, MC, AmEx

A popular and dramatic eatery for popular and dramatic people. The food is your typical international haute cuisine that relies more on atmosphere and less on actual flavour.

LUTTER & WEGNER

ⓘ Charlottenstrasse 56 ⓐ 2029 5410 ⏰ 11:00am–2:00am daily. ⓜ U-Bahn Stadtmitte ⓥ ⓒ V, MC, AmEx, DC

A historic landmark, Lutter & Wegner was originally a wine merchant specialising

Candles and columns at the Café Oren

in sparkling whites. This is where they coined the name *Sekt* to refer to German champagne. Central European and French dishes are well represented.

MARGAUX

🛈 Unter den Linden 78

🕾 2265 2611

🕒 Tues–Sat 12:00pm–2:00pm, 7:00pm– 10:30pm

🚇 S-Bahn Unter den Linden 🔞 🍴 V, MC, AmEx, DC

A temple to food, Margaux is named after the numerous bottles of Château Margaux on the wine list. Prices are expensive but the service, interiors and dishes more than make up for the damage to your wallet. Classic French is the restaurant's focus – and the final outcome is invariably excellent.

MAXWELL

🛈 Bergstrasse 22

🕾 280 7121 🕒 Summer 12:00pm–midnight daily; Winter 6:00pm–midnight daily. 🚇 U-Bahn Oranienburger Tor 🔞 🍴 V, MC, AmEx

Small portions, poor service and pretentiousness galore. That's the down side. Stunning artwork, a beautifully renovated brewery and a great

Seasons for stylish dining

summer patio. That's the up. Good, but not as good as the numerous other options in the immediate vicinity.

SEASONS

🛈 Charlottenstrasse 49

🕾 2033 6363

🕒 6:30am–10:30pm daily.

🚇 U-Bahn Stadtmitte

🔞 🍴 V, DC, AmEx

Nice international cuisine, including pasta and seafood dishes in the Four Seasons Hotel. Good value, even considering how much your final bill will probably be.

SOUL KITCHEN

🛈 Linienstrasse 136

🕾 2804 0362

🕒 5:00pm–1:00am daily.

🚇 U-Bahn Rosenthaler Platz 🔞 🍴–🍴 No credit cards

Momma never made cornbread this good!

Dig into African-American soul food usually found only in the backwoods of the Southern US. If you're like me you'll come back again and again if only to eat your weight in hush-puppies.

VAU

🛈 Jägerstrasse 54–5

🕾 202 9730

🕒 Mon–Sat 12:00pm–2:30pm, 7:00pm–midnight

🚇 U0Bahn Französische Strasse 🔞 🍴 full menu V, MC, AmEx, DC

International haute cuisine, particularly strong on seafood. Booking is recommended at this inspiring and intimate eatery. Just try and avoid the nasty wicker chairs and ugly 70s oils that draw the eye from the real artwork – the food on the plate.

PRENZLAUER BERG & FRIEDRICHS-HAIN

BANGKOK

- ℹ Prenzlauer Allee 46
- ☎ 443 9405
- ⏰ 11:00am–11:00pm daily.
- 💳 🎫 No credit cards

Local Thai dining spot with a South Seas beach hut feel to it. It's tiny, cramped and a bit off the culinary map, but makes no pretensions to be a five-star eatery.

MAO THAI

- ℹ Wörther Strasse 30
- ☎ 441 9261
- ⏰ Mon–Thurs, Sun 12:00pm–11:30pm; Fri–Sat 12:00pm–midnight
- 🚇 U-Bahn Senefelderplatz
- 💳 🎫 V, MC, AmEx, DC

One of the most popular "Thai" restaurants in town. Dishes are a bit more Chinese in flavour. Go to Bangkok for authenticity and Mao Thai for visual pleasure – the interiors are gorgeous.

OFFENBACH-STUBEN

- ℹ Stubbenkammerstrasse 8
- ☎ 445 8502
- ⏰ 6:00pm–2:00am daily.
- 🚇 S-Bahn Prenzlauer Allee
- 💳 🎫 No credit cards

Classic German food

in a restaurant that made its name before the wall came down as one of East Berlin's only privately-owned dining spots. The result is simple dining without the frills in a pleasing – if slightly odd – environment.

OXONMAGENTA

- ℹ Greifenhagener Strasse 48
- ☎ 4473 6482
- ⏰ 10:00am–late daily.
- 🚇 U-Bahn/S-Bahn Schönhauser Allee
- 💳 🎫 – 🎫 V, MC

Popular gay vegetarian and fish restaurant with a packed brunch every Sunday. Attracts a largely local crowd.

PASTERNAK

- ℹ Knaackstrasse 22–4
- ☎ 441 3399
- ⏰ 10:00am–2:00am daily.
- 🚇 U-Bahn Senefelderplatz
- 💳 🎫 No credit cards

Russian meals in an absolutely crammed dinery. If you can get the dreadful local musicians, constant bumping of tables and dreadful service out of your mind, then you'll enjoy the delicious *borscht* and stroganoffs on offer.

TRATTORIA PAPARAZZI

- ℹ Husemannstrasse 35
- ☎ 440 7333
- ⏰ 6:00pm–1:00am daily.

- 🚇 U-Bahn Eberswalder Strasse 🎫 🎫 – 🎫
- 💳 No credit cards.

The best Southern Italian food in town in a seemingly inconsequential restaurant. Okay, it may look like nothing much from the outside, but your mouth is sure to disagree with the visual blahness of it all.

VILLA GROTERJAN

- ℹ Milastrasse 2
- ☎ 440 6755
- ⏰ 12:00pm–1:00am daily.
- 🚇 U-Bahn/S-Bahn Schönhauser Allee
- 💳 🎫 No credit cards

Canteen-like East German restaurant that pulls in the punters primarily due to its stunning 1920s Old German architecture. Everything GDR from soup to schnitzel.

UMSPANNWERK OST

- ℹ Palisadenstrasse 48
- ☎ 4280 9497
- ⏰ 11:00am–late daily.
- 🚇 U-Bahn Weberwiese
- 💳 🎫 V, MC, AmEx, DC

Mediterranean dining in a restaurant converted from a transformer station originally built in 1900. Rough, industrial interiors make any eating experience here surprisingly elegant.

RESTAURANT FINDER

Pagoda flower power

American
Andy's Diner & Bar 45
Jimmy's Diner 85
Soul Kitchen 89
Café Nola 63

Australian
Woolloomooloo 84

French
Bistro Chez
  Maurice 55
La Cocotte 87
Margaux 89
Paris Bar 85

Gay Faves
Art 82
Café Berio 82
Café PositHIV 86
Lukiluki 84
Omnes 87
Oxonmagenta 90

German/ Austrian/Swiss
Altes Zollhaus 86
Austria 82
Bovril 25
Café Einstein 86
Fleischerei Bachhuber's
  bei Witty's 83
Florian 85
Grossbeerkeller 35
Ganymed 88
Gugelhof 55
Heinrich 85
Henne 87
Kellerrestaurant im
  Brecht-Haus 83
Marjellchen 85
Markthalle 87
Offenbach-Stuben 90

Tiergarten Quelle 63
Villa Groterjan 90

Imbiss/ Fast Food
Astor 45
Fish & Chips 35
Fritz & Co. 93
Konnopke's
Imbiss 55
Kulinarische
  Delikatessen 35
Marcann's 45
Safran 55
Spätzle 63

Indian/Sri- Lankan
Chandra Kumari 86
India Haus 87
Surya 25

International/ European
Adlon 81
Guy 88
Lutter & Wegner 88
Maxwell 89
Seasons 89
Umspannwerk Ost 90
Vau 89

Italian
Osteria No 1 88

Sale e Tabacchi 35
Trattoria Paparazzi 90

Lebanese
Mesa 85

Japanese
Kuchi 25
Sabu 84
Sachiko Sushi 86

Russian
Pasternak 90

Portuguese
Casa Portuguesa 63

Thai/Vietnamese /Cambodian
Bangkok 90
Mao Thai 90
Monsieur Vuong 45
Pagoda 88

Turkish Middle Eastern
Café Oren 88
Çardak 86
Habibi 86
Hasir 87

Vegetarian
Abendmahl 81
Hakuin 86

If the Wurst comes to the Wurst . . .

Sausages, Beer and Pretzels

The sausage is so integrally part of German culture that there are even sayings using the word wurst to describe one's emotions. Next time you encounter a German and you don't care about what they're saying, try responding with "It's all sausage to me" – *Mir ist alles Wurst*. They'll understand what you're trying to say (even if they don't quite appreciate how you're saying it). Berlin cuisine isn't the finest in Germany, but it is famous for drawing on the best the other parts of the country have to offer. The biggest contribution to *wurst* culture is the decidedly Berlin creation of the *currywurst*. Take one hot dog, grill it until cooked, sprinkle it with curry powder and lavish vast amounts of warm ketchup on it – and voila – you now have every Berliner's favourite fast food delight. Go to **Fritz & Co.** at Wittenbergplatz to give it a try. (*See p.25*.)

If you're confused by the array of sausages on offer, a good way to remember the differences is that *Weisswurst* and other white sausages are milder in flavour and tend to come from Bavaria and points south. Traditionally, they're also only eaten in the morning or "before the noon bells ring". Heartier, spicier varieties including *bratwurst* are eaten all day. And whatever you do, don't forget to put mustard on the thing or you'll be branded a stupid tourist.

Pretzels are another Berlin speciality. New Yorkers may be a bit confused when they see them, however, as they won't be dusted with the thick layer of salt commonly found on most Fifth Avenue street corners. German pretzels are sweeter in flavour and softer in texture than your average American twisty. Served with beer, they make for a nice change from peanuts and crisps.

Because of the poor growing conditions in surrounding fields, Berlin relies almost entirely on cabbage, potato and pork. Liver cooked with onions and apples is another speciality, albeit one that's hard to find in most restaurants.

Down it all with copious steins of beer. Local breweries aren't really known for their prowess. Berliner Pilsener is usually the brand of choice, on tap at most pubs and clubs. It's not the best German brew available on the market but it does the trick. Keep an eye out for Berlin's annual Oktoberfest beer tent held annually in the north of the city. It's not as famous as the one in Munich, but it'll quench your thirst for a good time.

Hidden attractions at Ficken 3000

Out on the Town

Sally Bowles described herself as being divinely decadent. The city of Berlin could say pretty much the same thing. This is a city of all-night clubbing, underground warehouse parties and writhing darkrooms. If sleeping all day and staying up all night is your idea of a good time, then you've come to the right place. In Berlin anything goes and the bars can stay open 24 hours a day if they want to – the question is, can you?

My Top Clubs

Café Melitta Sundström

🛈 Mehringdamm 61, Kreuzberg
📞 692 4414   🕙 10:00pm–late daily
Ⓤ U-Bahn Mehringdamm
🅒 No credit cards

The cosiest drinking spot on the Mehringdamm strip, Café Melitta Sundstrom is popular with a euro-funky coffee-imbibing kind of crowd. Perfect for a pre-clubbing chill-out or a lazy Sunday with friends, the place exudes a cosy warmth on even the grimmest of Berlin winter morns. It's a great place to kill a few hours with a newspaper and a few cigarettes. Everyone from drag queens to the "nobody knows I'm gay" set should feel right at home.

Die Busche

🛈 Mühlenstrasse 11–12, Friedrichshain
📞 296 0800   Ⓤ U-Bahn/S-Bahn
Warschauer Strasse   🅒 No credit cards

East Berlin's oldest gay club, Die Busche is an absolutely trippy experience that will have you reminiscing about your cousin's bar mitzvah or sister's wedding. Cheesy 80s hits and Ost-Rock one-hit wonders pump out of the deliberately dated sound system as the DJ dedicates every song to a miscellaneous bunch of mullet-clad lesbians or moustachioed gentlemen. He'll also talk through every song so don't bother trying to get into the groove of any track or you'll be disappointed. Majority lesbian, although gay men are allowed in if accompanied by a woman.

Ficken 3000

Indulgence

🛈 Urbanstrasse 70, Kreuzberg
📞 6950 7335
🕙 10:00pm–late daily.
🚇 U-Bahn Hermannplatz
💳 No credit cards

I went to Ficken 3000 expecting absolutely nothing. Go with no preconceptions and you'll have the best night of your vacation. Drag queens, gender-benders, local Turks and closet-cases populate this bar run by Berlin's leading Sister of Perpetual Indulgence – and what a stunner she is. Downstairs is an extremely cruisy darkroom frequented by one and all. Be careful walking down the narrow staircase – I almost fell head-first into what could only be described as an intimate moment of self-gratification.

Flax

🛈 Chodowieckistrasse 41, Prenzlauer Berg 📞 4404 6988 🕙 Mon–Fri 5:00pm–3:00am; Sat 3:00pm–3:00am; Sun 10:00am–3:00am
🚇 U-Bahn Eberswalder Strasse
💳 No credit cards

An intimate bar with candles on the tables and a welcoming feel. Drink specials are tacked up on chalkboards scattered throughout. It's a bit off the Prenzlauer Berg gay route, but worth the trek if you're looking for a nice place to enjoy a drink and actually have a discussion with new friends. Berlin bars are notorious for playing music at ear-shattering volume levels, making conversations almost impossible. This place doesn't follow that rule.

pe

🛈 Kalckreuthstrasse 10, Schöneberg
📞 218 7533
🕙 8:00pm–late daily
🚇 U-Bahn Nollendorfplatz
💳 No credit cards

Berlin's oldest lesbian bar – it now gets a bit of a bad rap from the local dyke community. pe was recently bought out by a minor German celebrity and transformed into a mixed venue. The management grudgingly open the bar to women-only on Saturdays – and this is the only day you should really check the place out. Any other time will see desperate crowds of ladies reminiscing about the old days.

Prinzknecht

ℹ Fuggerstrasse 33, Schöneberg
📞 2362 7444   ⏱ 3:00pm–3:00am daily
Ⓜ U-Bahn Wittenbergplatz
💳 No credit cards

Some people hate Prinzknecht, but I actually enjoy it due to its being one of the most attitude-free bars in Schöneberg. Somewhat neighbourhoody, you get a wide selection of punters from ageing queens to Muscle Marys (complete with fluffy poodles on a leash) popping by for a quick drink. Vaulted ceilings and massive artwork on the walls can sometimes work against the place, making it feel completely empty on nights when it's actually quite packed. Hit or miss.

Roses

ℹ Oranienstrasse 187, Kreuzberg
📞 615 6570   ⏱ 10:00pm–5:00am daily
Ⓜ U-Bahn Kottbusser Tor
💳 No credit cards

My absolutely, positively favourite gay and lesbian bar in Berlin. Of course, it's also everyone else's favourite bar too. The place is always heaving no matter what day of the week it is. The staff are friendly. The drink measures are massive. The décor is surreally amazing and it's entirely mixed between lesbians and gays, so everyone and anyone is welcome. Get here early if you want to snag a seat. It's a tiny venue so claustrophobics may feel uncomfortable.

Enjoy a refreshing drink at Prinzknecht

Bright lights of Bierhimmel

SchwuZ

🛈 Mehringdamm 61, Kreuzberg

🕿 693 7025 www.schwuz.de

✸ 11:00pm-late Fri–Sat

🚇 U-Bahn Mehringdamm

💳 Admission €4–€7.50. No credit cards

Berlin's longest running gay dance club and community institution, SchwuZ hosts tons of events, parties and nights of pleasure catering to almost every whim. One night will see the place taken over by techno freaks. The next could be an open-air sex party. You just never know what you'll find. Saturdays boast a popular disco evening that takes over much of the courtyard and two floors of fun. The weekly Safer-Sex-Party featuring a Roman orgy theme is legendary.

Tom's Bar

🛈 Motzstrasse 19, Schöneberg

🕿 213 4570 www.tomsbar.de

✸ Mon–Thurs, Sun 10:00pm–6:00am; Fri–Sat 10:00pm–late

🚇 U-Bahn Nollendorfplatz

💳 No credit cards

The cruisiest bar in Berlin (at least the cruisiest one that isn't classified as a sex-on-premises venue), Tom's Bar is the most popular bar in Schöneberg. The place opens simply enough. Buzz the bell at the door, walk in, check your coat and settle in for a beer. The further you go towards the rear, however, the more the temperature rises. Pretty soon you may have to ask your new friends if that's a beer bottle they're holding or if they're just happy to see you.

All Clubbed Out

ACKERKELLER

ⓘ Ackerstrasse 12 hinterhof, Mitte 🕾 280 7216 🕙 Tues 10:00pm–3:00am; Fri 10:00pm–late 🚇 S-Bahn Nordbahnhof 🎟 Admission €2. No credit cards

A great indie and underground club that plays punk, industrial, and Brit pop to an adoring crowd of mixed students. Just don't do what I did and go on German polka night.

ANDERES UFER

ⓘ Hauptstrasse 157, Schöneberg 🕾 784 1578 🕙 Mon–Fri 9:00am–2:00am 🚇 U-Bahn Kleistpark 🎟 No credit cards

The city's oldest gay bar, it can also boast the oldest drinkers in Berlin. Not exactly home to a pumping crowd of youngsters, the team of lesbians and gay men who ` run the place have attempted to maintain the alternative leanings of the place with regular art exhibitions and photography.

BARBIE BAR

ⓘ Mehringdamm 77, Kreuzberg 🕾 6956 8610 🕙 4:00pm–late daily 🚇 U-Bahn Mehringdamm 🎟 No credit cards

Camp little drinking spot the size of a shoebox. A nice place to start your evening or for a quiet drink on weekdays. Barbie Bar can feel dead on some nights so it's best to have a few other options at the ready in case the crowd disappoints.

BARGELB

ⓘ Mehringdamm 62, Kreuzberg 🕾 7889 9299 www.bargelb.de 🕙 8:00pm–late daily 🚇 U-Bahn Mehringdamm 🎟 No credit cards

Another tiny boîte on Mehringdamm. A good bar to wind down in after a long night of clubbing, thanks to its late closing times.

BIERHIMMEL

ⓘ Oranienstrasse 183, Kreuzberg 🕾 615 3122 🕙 1:00pm–3:00am daily 🚇 U-Bahn Kottbusser Tor 🎟 No credit cards

The Roses alternative in Kreuzberg. Slightly cooler, yet not as popular – local drag queens like to call this place home. Straight and gay friendly.

CAFÉ AMSTERDAM

ℹ️ Gleimstrasse 24, Prenzlauer Berg

📞 448 0792

www.pension-amsterdam.de

🕐 Mon–Thurs 9:00am–3:00am; Fri–Sat 9:00am–5:00am; Sun 9:00am–3:00am

🚇 U-Bahn/S-Bahn Schönhauser Allee

💳 No credit cards

Minimalist little café in Prenzlauer Berg. Slightly snotty staff make it a bit of an annoyance. Mixed crowd catered to. Snacks are served in case you have the munchies.

CLUB 69/GAYMEBOYS

ℹ️ Kalkscheune, Johannisstrasse 2, Mitte

📞 2839 0065

www.dissentertainment.de

🕐 Club 69 11:00pm–late, GaymeBoys 9:30pm–late one Sat per month. Phone ahead for details.

🚇 U-Bahn Oranienburger Tor 💳 Admission €5–€9 No credit cards

Good news for you chickens – here is a club for youngsters. You have to be 26 or under to get in. A great place for toddlers just coming out or prematurely jaded by the gay scene. And yes they will card you to ensure you're the age you say you are.

CRISCO

ℹ️ Nollendorfstrasse 27, Schöneberg

📞 2101 4020

🕐 Mon–Thurs 9:00pm–4:00am; Fri-Sat 9:00pm–late; Sun 6:00pm– late

🚇 U-Bahn Nollendorfplatz

💳 No credit cards

Hard-core fetish bar for hard-core leather and uniform lovers.

CONNECTION

ℹ️ Fuggerstrasse 33, Schöneberg

📞 218 1432

www.connection-berlin.com

🕐 Fri-Sat 10:00pm–7:00am

🚇 U-Bahn Wittenbergplatz

💳 €6 Admission (includes one free drink) No credit cards

A bit out of date no matter how hard it tries, men-only

Saturdays are the reason for this bar's existence. A vast darkroom often lures many an unsuspecting soul off the dance floor.

DANCE WITH THE ALIENS

ℹ️ Ostgut, Mühlenstrasse 26-30, Friedrichshain

📞 No phone

www.ostgut.de

🕐 3rd Fri of each month 11:00pm–late

🚇 S-Bahn Ostbahnhof

💳 Admission €10. No credit cards

A wild club for lesbians, gay men and friends. Want to dance naked? Go right ahead. Feel like going to a darkroom? There are three on offer – one for lesbians, one for gay men and one for..well…anyone else. Only held on the third Friday of each month.

Crisco leather fetish bar

OUT ON THE TOWN

DARKROOM

🛈 Rodenbergstrasse 23, Prenzlauer Berg

🌀 444 9321

www.darkroom–berlin.de

🌙 10:00pm–5:00am daily

Ⓜ U-Bahn/S-Bahn Schönhauser Allee

🚫 No credit cards

Tiny dark bar with a darkroom. Couldn't you tell by the name? What did you expect – a cocktail lounge?

GREIFBAR

🛈 Wichertstrasse 10, Prenzlauer Berg

🌀 444 0828

🌙 10:00pm–6:00am daily

Ⓜ VU-Bahn/S-Bahn Schönhauser Allee

🚫 No credit cards

Another bar with a darkroom a mere five steps from Darkroom. This one has a bit of an industrial feel to it.

GOLDRAUSCH

🛈 Rosenthaler Strasse 72A, Mitte 🌀 No phone

🌙 6:00pm–late daily

Ⓜ U-Bahn Rosenthaler Platz 🚫 No credit cards

Owned and operated by the people who brought you Roses, Goldrausch is one of the most visually inspiring bars in Berlin. A former Burger King, you'd never be able to tell that Whoppers were once sold in this gilt-laden masterpiece. Mixed.

HAFEN

🛈 Motzstrasse 19, Schöneberg

🌀 211 4118

🌙 8:00pm–late daily

Ⓜ U-Bahn Nollendorfplatz

🚫 No credit cards

Supposedly this place is popular but each time I go it's absolutely dead. Summers are the time to hit when the windows open up and it becomes people-watching central.

HOUSE BOYS

🛈 Kalkscheune, Johannisstrasse 2, Mitte

🌀 2839 0065

www.dissentertainment.de

🌙 11:00pm–late, no fixed dates. Call ahead for details

Ⓜ U-Bahn Oranienburger Tor

🚫 €5–€9. No credit cards

Great house music and wild clothes for a young crowd. If you have but one wrinkle on your face, you may feel like an unwanted grandfather.

KLUB INTERNATIONAL

🛈 c/o Kino International, Karl-Marx-Allee 33, Mitte

🌀 2475 6011

🌙 1st Sat of each month 11:00pm–late

Ⓜ U-Bahn Schillingstrasse

🚫 €8. No credit cards

The largest gay club in Berlin. 1,500 up-for-it clubbers can – and often do – pack into this former GDR cinema built in the 50s. The current craze for anything Iron Curtain makes it architecturally fascinating and entirely chic.

Cosy cocktails

Poster promises

PICK AB!

ⓘ Greifenhagener
Strasse 16,
Prenzlauer Berg

☎ 445 8523

🕙 10:00pm–6:00am
daily.

Ⓜ U-Bahn/S-Bahn
Schönhauser Allee

Ⓥ No credit cards

Yet another
Prenzlauer Berg
bar with a darkroom.
This darkroom is
minute in size.
Slightly more
camp in flavour
than the other
darkroom-focused
bars in the immediate
vicinity.

SO 36

ⓘ Oranienstrasse
190, Kreuzberg

☎ 6140 1306

www.so36.de

🕙 Mon, Wed
10:00pm–late

Ⓜ U-Bahn Kottbusser Tor

Ⓥ €5. No credit cards

A popular venue for
both gay men and
lesbians with booming
events on Mondays
(hard techno) and
Wednesdays (slightly
softer house with
more lesbian
interaction). The last
Saturday of each
month caters to gay
Turks and comes

complete with belly
dancers and Turkish
pop music.

STILLER DON

ⓘ Erich-Weinert-Strasse
67, Prenzlauer Berg

☎ 445 5957

www.stillerdon.de

🕙 8:00pm–4:00am
daily

Ⓜ U-Bahn/S-Bahn
Schönhauser Allee

Ⓥ No credit cards

An artsy café/bar
with an intellectual
feel. Draped red
velvet and dark wood
add to the dramatic
atmosphere.

Doris Disse & Ken Mattel bring you:

ouseBoys

The Love Parade!

By the time you read this, the Love Parade could either be a distant memory or it may continue to be Berlin's biggest party of the year. No one ever really knows if the thing is going to go on until the last possible minute – but it invariably does go ahead in some shape or form.

So what is it then? Well, that's hard to explain. Founded in 1989 as a response to the fall of communism, the Love Parade is a mass explosion of music, dancing, drinking and drugging that takes over Tiergarten for a single July weekend. Originally attracting only 350 partygoers, over a million people now descend on the German capital each year to take part in the debauched proceedings. The crush of human bodies is overwhelming.

Techno, drum 'n' bass, African drumming, trance, deep house, garage, disco – if it's playing the clubs then it'll be playing here in a raucously loud mishmash of floats and dance spaces. Grumbling abounds that the parade has lost its way from its original roots as a political demonstration. The commercialism that has clearly infiltrated proceedings is obvious. But when you're talking about a party the size of your average Midwestern city, you don't really care if everything is sponsored by a major multinational as long as someone else is in charge of cleaning up.

Environmentalists hate the thing, claiming that the event is doing untold damage to Tiergarten – and you can't really blame them, considering the volume of waste and puddles of urine that cover the park for days after the parade has been and gone.

The parade route has remained pretty much the same since its early days, beginning at the Brandenburger Tor and running along Strasse des 17 Juni.

To make the day a success, bring plenty of sunscreen, water, food and a mobile telephone to keep in contact with friends. No matter how hard you try you are guaranteed to lose anyone you come to the event with, you will have to give in and pee on the street at some point due to the chronic lack of toilet facilities; you will pay through the nose for a limp sausage; your beer will be warm and expensive; you'll probably get more than a grope from a random stranger in full view of hundreds of people – and no one will look or care as they'll be too busy stumbling around the dozens of other fornicators littering the various meadows and shaded corners.

Philharmonie – home of the world famous Berlin Philharmonic Orchestra

Playing Around Town

Berlin is a culture vulture's paradise. From theatre to classical music, opera to dance, the city boasts some of the world's finest venues and artists. Berliners take their arts scene seriously and would never forgive their government if they considered cutting the generous subsidies and grants that the companies rely on. In this town, a night at the opera is still something of an event so your tux should be well-pressed if you're considering an evening of Puccini. Tickets are like gold dust for pretty much everything in town, so be sure to book well in advance for the big names.

OUTLINES

BERLINER ENSEMBLE

🛈 Bertolt-Brecht-Platz 1, Mitte

📞 282 3160/2840 8155 www.berliner-ensemble.de

🎭 Box Office Mon–Sat 8:00am–6:00pm; Sun 11:00am–6:00pm

Ⓤ U-Bahn/S-Bahn Friedrichstrasse

💳 V, MC, AmEx

The house that Bertolt Brecht built, the Berliner Ensemble is the jewel in Berlin's theatrical crown. This is the theatre that saw the premiere of Brecht's earliest works before his self-imposed exile in America. The season now includes works from other playwrights, but this is only a recent convention. All works are performed in German.

DEUTSCHE OPER

🛈 Bismarckstrasse 35, Charlottenburg

📞 343 8401/0800 248 9842 www.deutsche-oper.berlin.de 🎭 Box Office Mon–Fri 11:00am–7:00pm; Sat 10:00am–2:00pm

Ⓤ U-Bahn Deutsche Oper

💳 V, AmEx, DC

A monolithic 1,900 - seat opera hall that plays second fiddle to the grander and more centrally located Staatsoper. Known for its 19th century blockbusters, you can often find seats available here when other venues are sold out.

DEUTSCHES THEATER

🛈 Schumannstrasse 13A, Mitte

📞 Box Office 2844 1225/Info 2844 1222 www.deutsches-theater.berlin.net

🎭 Box Office Mon–Sat 11:00am–6:30pm; Sun 3:00pm–6:30pm

Ⓤ U-Bahn/S-Bahn Friedrichstrasse

💳 V, MC, AmEx

Young directors, fresh

The imposing Konzerthaus

talent and West End theatrical hits perform here – albeit strictly in German. Visionary artistic direction means that you often get to see some innovative stuff.

FRIENDS OF ITALIAN OPERA

ⓘ Fidicinstrasse 40, Kreuzberg

🚗 Box Office 691 1211/Info 693 5692

www.thefriends.de

😊 Varies

🚇 U-Bahn Platz der Luftbrücke

💳 No credit cards

The only English-language theatre in the city. Productions here can sometimes have a bit of a community theatre feel to them. The company specialises in fringe productions and in producing visiting

performers and companies, so you won't be seeing too much in the way of native talent.

KOMISCHE OPER

ⓘ Behrenstrasse 55–7, Mitte

🚗 202 600/4799 7400

www.komische-oper-berlin.de

😊 Box Office Sun 11:00am–7:00pm; Sun 1:00pm–1hr before performance

🚇 S-Bahn Unter den Linden

💳 V, MC, AmEx, DC

A small opera house with a focus more on theatrical performance than on voice quality. That's not to say you'll be getting second-rate singers, rather, the Komische Oper strives to create complete works of art that demand total

performances from their company. The results are often ten times more satisfying than the stuff you find on the five-star stages.

KONZERTHAUS

ⓘ Gendarmenmarkt 2, Mitte

🚗 2030 92101

www.konzerthaus.de

😊 Box Office Mon–Sat 12:00pm–7:00pm; Sun 12:00pm–4:00pm

🚇 U-Bahn Französische Strasse

💳 V, MC, AmEx

The best concert hall in town, the Konzerthaus is a bit like London's Royal Albert Hall in the fact that it doesn't call itself home to a single group or company. Everything from organ recitals to symphony performances is on offer depending on who books the place out. Contemporary music is a speciality.

PHILHARMONIE

ⓘ Herbert-von-Karajan Strasse 1, Tiergarten

🚗 2548 8126

www.berlin-philharmonie.com

😊 Box Office Mon–Fri 3:00pm–6:00pm; Sat–Sun 11:00am–2:00pm

🚇 U-Bahn/S-Bahn Potsdamer Platz

💳 V, MC, AmEx

The home of the

world-renowned Berlin Philharmonic Orchestra, the Philharmonie is probably the most difficult place to get your hands on tickets. Performances here are society events entailing much flashing of designer duds and schmoozing amongst Berlin's elite. And for good reason. The music that emanates from this place is sublime – especially under the exciting artistic direction of conductor and enfant terrible Sir Simon Rattle.

STAATSOPER UNTER DEN LINDEN

Unter den Linden 5–7, Mitte

203 540/tickets 2035 4555

www.staatsoper-berlin.org

Box Office Mon–Fri 10:00am–8:00pm; Sat-Sun 2:00pm–8:00pm

U-Bahn Hausvogteiplatz

V, MC, AmEx

The Staatsoper is the grande dame of opera halls in Berlin. Founded as the Royal Court Opera for Frederick the Great in 1742, the building is designed to resemble a Greek temple. Many have worshipped at the Staatsoper, with its beautiful interiors and the sense of history that seems to ooze from every corner. Music maestro Daniel Barenboim is the current director of the resident company. If you're willing to chance it, you can score €10 tickets half-an-hour before the performance if any remain unsold.

TACHELES

Oranienburger Strasse 54–6, Mitte

2809 6123

www.tacheles.de

Varies

U-Bahn Oranienburger Tor   No credit cards

Tacheles is Berlin's leading alternative fringe venue hosting everything from new age dance to post-Wall political theatre. Underground art is its reason for existence so you can either catch something exhilarating or catch a disease from the various unwashed personae next to you, depending on what's on stage. Some productions are performed in English.

THEATER AM KURFÜRSTENDAMM

Kurfürstendamm 206-9, Charlottenburg

4799 7440

www.theater-des-westens.de

Box Office Mon–Sat 11:00am–7:00pm; Sun 11:00am–2:00pm

U-Bahn/S-Bahn Zoologischer Garten

V, MC, AmEx

Berlin's big touring house venue for largescale plays and mega-musicals. Most of the productions are in German featuring b-list Teutonic stars whom you'll probably never have heard of.

Amici dell' Opera

Cabaret/
Isherwood

Wilkommen! Bienvenus! Welcome! If you're anything like me then your first pangs of desire to visit Berlin occurred when you saw Liza Minnelli belt out her Oscar-winning performance in the film *Cabaret*. The 1972 celluloid sensation, which saw Ms. Minnelli play the character of Sally Bowles, was an international smash, featuring brilliant music from the hands of John Kander and Fred Ebb. In addition to capturing the hearts of critics worldwide, *Cabaret* introduced the world to the stages of 1930s Germany and transformed its cast and director Bob Fosse into global sensations.

But the film was not the first medium in which divinely decadent nightclub singer Sally Bowles made an appearance. In addition to the stage musical *Cabaret* from which the film was loosely derived, the themes and story of *Cabaret* first saw light in the works of British novelist Christopher Isherwood.

Isherwood, an out homosexual (well, mostly out, that is), introduced Sally Bowles to an unsuspecting planet in his 1939 collection of short stories entitled *Goodbye to Berlin*. Somewhat autobiographical, *Goodbye to Berlin* is one of the best and most insightfully written books about the city and its perilous descent into National Socialism. It's also a great read.

A fixture on the gay circuit of the 30s, Isherwood was a regular partygoer in the bars and clubs of Nollendorfplatz. Amongst his close friends was an up-and-coming young starlet known as Marlene Dietrich – soon to make it big in Hollywood. You can still see the house in which he lived at Nollendorfstrasse 17. Unfortunately, as it is a residential home, you can't go inside.

In its heyday, cabaret was one of Berlin's most popular nights out. Political satire, singing, dancing and ribald jokes made for a full evening of entertainment. Since it was catering to the masses, it was usually cheap. Nazis hated the world of cabaret as it was usually owned, operated and performed by Jews, homosexuals and communists – or a combination of all three. Most of the venues were shut down by the time World War II broke out and never regained their initial success.

Today's cabarets are more like variety shows, either geared towards a tourist crowd, relying heavily on transvestites or looking a bit like mini-circuses. While you probably won't see exactly what you're looking for (no greasy emcees singing about a *ménage à trois* or jaded dancing girls here), you'll probably still have a good time – as long as you understand German. English speakers may find

Remembering Mr. Issyvoo

everything a tad confusing, except in some of the bigger and more commercial venues like Pomp, Duck and Circumstance. Some of the better cabaret options in Berlin can be found below.

ISHERWOOD'S HOME

- ℹ Nollendorfstrasse 17, Schöneberg
- No phone
- 24hrs daily (It's a residential home)
- U-Bahn Nollendorfplatz

BAR JEDER VERNUNFT

- ℹ Schaperstrasse 24, Wilmersdorf
- 883 1582
- www.bar-jeder-vernunft.de
- Box Office 12:00pm–7:00pm daily
- U-Bahn Spichernstrasse
- V, MC

CHAMÄLEON VARIETÉ

- ℹ Hackesche Höfe, Rosenthaler Strasse 40–41, Mitte 282 7118
- www.chamaeleonberlin.de
- Box Office Mon–Thurs, 12:00pm–9:00pm; Fri–Sat 12:00pm–midnight;

Sun 4:00pm–9:00pm
- S-Bahn Hackescher Markt No credit cards

CHEZ NOUS

- ℹ Marburger Strasse 14, Charlottenburg
- 213 1810
- Box Office Mon–Sat 10:00am–1:00pm, 1:30pm–6:30pm
- U-Bahn/S-Bahn Zoologischer Garten
- No credit cards

KLEINE NACHTREVUE

- ℹ Kurfürstenstrasse 16, Schöneberg
- 218 8950
- Box Office Mon–Sat 9:00pm–4:00am
- U-Bahn Wittenbergplatz
- V, AmEx, DC

POMP, DUCK AND CIRCUMSTANCE

- ℹ Möckrenstrasse 26, Kreuzberg
- 2694 9200

www.pompduck.de
- Box Office Tues–Sat 6:00pm–midnight; Sun 5:00pm–11:00pm
- U-Bahn Möckrenbrücke
- MC

ROTER SALON/GRÜNER SALON

- ℹ Rosa-Luxemburg-Platz, Mitte
- 247 6772
- Varies
- U-Bahn Rosa-Luxemburg-Platz
- No credit cards

WINTERGARTEN VARIETÉ

- ℹ Potsdamer Strasse 96, Tiergarten
- 250 0880/Info 2500 8888
- Box Office 10:00am–curtain daily
- U-Bahn Kurfürstendamm
- V, MC, AmEx

STEA

SAUNA CLUB BERLIN KURFÜRSTENSTR. 113

SAUNA

TEAM
OOM

M
OOM

ING &
NDREASKREUZ

WIEDERERÖFFNUN
am Donnerstag
22.August 14.00 U

VHI
OO

CLARIUM

Working Out

Germans are a healthy sort. Neither the gym bunnies of America nor the pasty sticks of Britain, locals maintain an active lifestyle and love of nature that is unsurpassed. Rather than spend hours in an airless weights room, Berliners spend their free time enjoying city parkland, cycling through Tiergarten, swimming in the numerous lakes that circle the city and making good use of the dozens of saunas that can be found all over town – although a good steam may not be the number-one reason why the saunas have proven to be so popular. That's not to say that you won't find any Muscle Marys in this town. Lovers of a good gluteus maximus and perfect pecs won't be disappointed.

OUTLINES

APOLLO CITY SAUNA

🛈 Kurfürstenstrasse 101, Tiergarten

🖥 213 2424

🕙 1:00pm–7:00am daily

🚇 U-Bahn Wittenbergplatz

💳 €13–€17. No credit cards

One of Berlin's largest saunas, the Apollo City Sauna is a steamy mass of sin and sex boasting 130 lockers and 60 cabins open to the masses of men who crawl through the place on a daily basis. Weekdays can feel a bit dead, but there's always plenty of action going on.

Don't worry if they're sold out of cabins – as they often are on weekends – there are still plenty of steam rooms, porn video nooks, and a weights room.

AQUARIUM MENFITNESS

🛈 Wilmersdorfer Strasse 82/83, Charlotten

🖥 324 1025

www.aquarius-berlin.de

🕙 Mon, Wed, Fri; 10:00am–11:00pm; Tues, Thurs 7:00am–11:00pm; Sat–Sun 7:00am–11:00pm

🚇 U-Bahn Adenauerplatz

🛈 Day and month rates

💳 available starting at €10. V, MC, AmEx, DC

A men-only gym in West Charlottenburg. While not strictly gay, the majority of its members are of a pink persuasion. Well equipped, with all of the weights and cardio machines you might need to stay fit, there's also an extensive range of classes to choose from if you're looking to try something new.

AXXEL CITY FITNESS

🛈 Bülowstrasse 57, Schöneberg

🖥 2175 3000

www.axxel24.de

🕙 24hrs daily.

🚇 U-Bahn Bülowstrasse

Time for some sport

 Rates available starting at €25.

No credit cards

Can't sleep? Why not work your insomnia out at Berlin's only 24-hour fitness centre. The place has everything you might need to give your muscles a run for their money. You'll be surprised just how many other people in this all-night town decide to join you for a cardio-bike session at 4:00am. Men and women welcome.

GATE SAUNA

 Wilhelmstrasse 81, Mitte  229 9430
www.gate-sauna.de
 Mon–Thurs 11:00am–7:00am; non-stop Fri 11:00am–Mon7:00am
 S-Bahn Unter den Linden  €12–€20. No credit cards

The neighbourhood sauna for Mitte, the Gate is decidedly more adult in tone, even though it markets itself to all ages. Nights for bears, fetishists and SM lovers are frequent and there is a sling available in the basement should you need one.

STEAM SAUNA

 Kurfürstenstrasse 113, Tiergarten  218 4060
www.steam-sauna.de
 Mon–Thurs11:00am–7:00am; non-stop Fri 11:00am –Mon7:00am
 U-Bahn Wittenbergplatz
 €14. No credit cards

Across the street from the Apollo City, Steam Sauna is the second choice for those looking for a bit of action. Saturdays are often packed with locals and clubbers looking to stretch

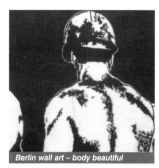

Berlin wall art – body beautiful

their weekends as long as they can.

STRANDBAD MÜGGELSEE

ℹ️ Fürstenwalder Damm 838, Rahnsdorf

📞 648 7777 🚇 S-Bahn Rahnsdorf 🕐 Call for details. No credit cards

An outdoor bathing beach on the banks of East Berlin's largest lake. A nudist camp is available if you want to let it all hang out. Popular on sunny days and weekends.

TREIBHAUS SAUNA

ℹ️ Schönhauser Allee 132, Prenzlauer Berg

📞 448 4503
www.treibhaussauna.de
🕐 Mon–Thurs

1:00pm–7:00am; non-stop Fri 11:00am–Mon 7:00am 🚇 U-Bahn Eberswalder Strasse 💳 €14.50–€20 (including drink ticket). No credit cards

The hip sauna for the Prenzlauer Berg set, Treibhaus tends to attract the youngest and cutest sauna-going scenesters due to their cut-rate student prices. Pretty much the same facilities all the other saunas have, except slightly smaller in size. In case you get lost, the entrance is through the courtyard.

Sin and sauna

Sex Party Scene

Say to a German that you got laid the night before and chances are you'll get a look of blasé disinterest. Berlin isn't exactly the most difficult town in which to dip your wick or tip the velvet. Ten years ago when other cities were telling residents to stay in their bedrooms with a nice bit of porn and a practised five-fingered shuffle (or dildo for the ladies – don't worry, I haven't forgotten you), Berlin responded by opening up dozens of sex clubs, fetish parties and SM parlours for one and all. If you're shocked by the sight of a bit of open-air oral or a naked dance-floor tango, then you might want to flip through the next page or two – we're about to get a little dirty here.

And now for something completely different . . .

Time to dress

AJPNIA

🛈 Eisenacher Strasse 23, Schöneberg

📞 2191 8881

www.ajpnia.de

☀ 9:00pm–late Sat

🚇 U-Bahn Nollendorfplatz

💳 €5–€6. No credit cards

A men-only sex party held on Saturdays. Nachtverkehr positHIV, held the first and third Saturday of each month, is for HIV-positive patrons only. The other Saturdays are more your general, everyday orgy. No shrinking violets allowed.

BODIES IN MOTION @ AHA

🛈 Mehringdamm 61, Kreuzberg

📞 692 3600

www.aha-berlin.de

☀ every 2nd Fri 9:00am–5:00am

🚇 U-Bahn Mehringdamm

💳 €6. No credit cards

A volunteer-run fundraiser for the AHA centre, Bodies in Motion is the sex party that started it all. Due to its location in a community centre, the atmosphere is extremely relaxed and very young. Mattresses line the floor as curtains partition off the tiny space in special alcoves of pleasure. The best of the non-SM options. Men only.

BÖSE BUBEN

🛈 Lichtenrader Strasse 32, 2nd hinterhof, Neukölln

📞 6270 5610

www.boesebubenberlin.de

☀ Wed 5:30pm–10:00pm; Fri-Sat 9:00pm–midnight

🚇 U-Bahn Leinestrasse

💳 €5. No credit cards

Medieval-style interiors and some of the friendliest staff in Berlin provide a welcoming environment for fans of pain with their pleasure. The playroom is extraordinarily well-equipped with cages, racks, chains, restraints, crosses and slings. A "hospital" room caters to fans of doctor/patient fetishes. Young and old mix and mingle happily. Last time I was here I saw a 23-year-old Adonis happily flaying an 80-year-old gentleman with his "piece". Men only.

KITKATCLUB

🛈 Bessemerstrasse 2, Schöneberg

www.kitkatclub.de

☀ 1st Fri of each month 9:00pm–late

🚇 S-Bahn Papestrasse

💳 €5–€10. No credit cards

I've been around the block but even I was shocked by the goings on at the KitKatClub. More decadent by far than the one in the movie, the KitKat welcomes gays and straights to its exotic fetish orgies. On some nights it's hard to weave your way through the copulating couples. Dress to impress – a fetish code is strictly enforced and only the beautiful will get past the selective bouncers. The first Monday of the month is gay-only. Lesbians and gay men welcome.

You can keep your hat on

WORKING OUT

LAB.ORATORY

ℹ️ Mühlenstrasse 26–30, Friedrichshain
📞 290 0579
www.lab-oratory.de
🕐 Varies
Ⓜ️ U-Bahn/S-Bahn Warschauer Strasse
💳 €4–€5. No credit cards

A gay hard-core disco for the discerning pervert. Intensely dark, Lab reserves weekends for fetish parties. Men only.

QUÄLGEIST

ℹ️ Kortestrasse 15–17, 2nd hinterhof, Kreuzberg
🕐 Fri, Sat 10:00pm–late

Ⓜ️ U-Bahn Südstern
💳 €8–€15. No credit cards

The first SM club in town, it's not as friendly as Böse Buben nor as well-maintained. A strict dress code separates the curious from the converts. Occasional beginner classes are offered throughout the year in addition to bondage, slave and fist nights. Men only.

STAHLROHR

ℹ️ Greifenhagener Strasse 54, Prenzlauer Berg

📞 473 2747
🕐 10:00am–6:00am daily
Ⓜ️ U-Bahn/S-Bahn Schönhauser Allee
💳 €7. No credit cards

A neighbourhood-style hard-core bar with a massive darkroom. Sort of what you would picture Cheers to be like if everyone dropped on their knees and started copulating every five minutes. Sunday afternoons are very popular, serving up coffee and cakes to attendees. Men only.

For the party animal

blue Movie

SANS. SOUCI.

Sanssouci Palace, Potsdam

Out of Town

With its amazing rail connections and strong infrastructure, daytrips and longer weekends out of Berlin are extremely easy to plan. The sights to see within a few hours of the capital are numerous, ranging from devastating memorials to the victims of Nazi Germany to grand palaces of Kaiser-filled days gone by. Three of the most popular options are Sachsenhausen, Potsdam and Leipzig, although more adventurous types could go as far as Prague and Hamburg – both are within a six-to-eight hour journey from the city.

Leipzig

East Germany's second city fell to ruin under the beleaguered leadership of the GDR government. Investment and western business is helping the city battle back from its smog-filled past, but there's still a bit of work left to do. Home-town of Johann Sebastian Bach, Leipzig has long been considered a centre for education and culture. It was here that the seeds of rebellion against Soviet control were first sown.

Trade fairs are what bring the masses into Leipzig, with shows dedicated to everything from books to toys. The shows pack city hotels for weeks of schmoozing and handshaking every year. In fact, it was at the 1902 Leipzig toy fair where a little stuffed bear was exhibited to the world by the Steiff toy company, sparking the international craze for the teddy bear.

Situated 130 kilometres south-west of Berlin, getting here is a breeze. The city centre is easy to navigate due to its compact size. Make your first stop the Markt (old market square) to explore the Old Town Hall, Königshaus (Saxon royal residence) and Town Museum. Just off the south-west corner of the square you will find the Thomaskirche, the home of Bach for the 27 years he spent in the city as choirmaster of the Thomas' Boys Choir. You will find his grave in the chancel and a large statue outside the main entrance.

Immediately behind the Altes Rathaus (old town hall) is the Old Stock Exchange, built in 1687. You'll spot it by the statue of favourite son and noted academic, Goethe, in front of its quaint doors.

Mädler Passage is a beautiful shopping arcade worth checking out, if only to admire the architecture that houses the cute, crafty shops located inside.

South of Thomaskirche is the New Town Hall – ironically named since the site can be traced back to the 16th century.

Other spots worth a look-see include the Museum of Arts Picture

Gallery for its collection of Old Masters, Leipzig University (alumni include Wagner, Schumann and the aforementioned Goethe) and the fascinating Museum in der 'Runde Ecke' with its displays of all things *Stasi*, including jars that collected the scent and body odour of suspected enemies of the state.

Leipzig Marketplatz

HOW TO GET THERE

Direct trains from Berlin take about two hours. Trains depart from both Ostbahnhof and Zoo station regularly.

Potsdam

The capital of Brandenburg, Potsdam is Berlin's Versailles – a collection of splendid royal palaces, residences and parks that speak of a time when the Prussian Empire ruled much of Central Europe. Summer weekends draw huge crowds to Park Sanssouci and the baroque town centre. The park boasts a wonderful collection of palaces and buildings built in the baroque style. Absolutely heaving on weekends, the main draw is Schloss Sanssouci ("without cares") – and, boy, if you lived in a place like this you wouldn't have any cares either... except perhaps how to pay the heating bill. Frederick the Great built the gardens here in 1740.

The first palace built on the grounds, and the one to give the entire complex its name, is the semicircular building at the top of the terrace, now housing a collection of paintings.

Other palaces and noted structures to check out include the Neues Palais built between 1763 to 1769 to commemorate the end of the Seven Years War, the Japanese-feeling Drachenhaus coffee shop, the Chinesisches Teehaus (Chinese teahouse) with its holdings of Asian and German porcelain, the sprawling Orangerie, the children's playhouse – the Spielfestung complete with fully-working toy cannons and the imitation Roman villa, the Römischer Bäder.

A short jaunt from the park is Alexandrowa, a faux-Russian village built to house court musicians shipped in from the Russian Empire, and prisoners of war.

War buffs may want to go even further outside of town with a visit to Schloss Cecilienhof, the last castle to be built in Potsdam, completed in 1917. It was in these grounds that the Potsdam Conference took place between Stalin, Truman and Attlee, carving up post-war Germany between the three superpowers.

While the actual town was almost bombed into rubble in 1945, the town centre and Altes Rathaus still hold a few attractions for fans of baroque architecture. Don't be dissuaded by the massive council flats that line the city as your train enters its destination. You have come to the right place. Just follow the crowds to the good stuff.

HOW TO GET THERE

Potsdam can be reached by S-Bahn using the S7 line. Taking around 40 minutes from Mitte, it can feel like a bit of a trek. Faster service is available on the regional trains from Zoo Station. Purchase a ticket to Potsdam Hauptbahnhof and see your journey time cut in half.

Sachsenhausen

The closest concentration camp to the city of Berlin, Sachsenhausen was used mainly as a holding pen for political prisoners and communist sympathisers. It opened in July 1936. Changes in policy meant that 6000 Jews were shipped here immediately following Kristallnacht and by 1945, 33,000 inmates were held within the camp. As the Russians approached the city, however, all of the prisoners were marched to the Baltic Sea, were loaded onto ships and sunk at sea. The only survivors were the 3000 or so "lucky ones" found in the camp hospital who were physically or mentally unable to embark on the trek. Sachsenhausen was liberated on 22 April 1945 and was one of the last camps to be captured by the Allies.

Unfortunately, Sachsenhausen's status as a political detention camp and centre for mass killing didn't end when World War II was won. The Russian secret police reopened Sachsenhausen and gave it the title of Camp 7. After the fall of the GDR government, a mass grave of over 10,000 bodies was found on the grounds.

Sachsenhausen was reopened one last time on 23 April 1961 as a national memorial, with a museum and memorial hall/cinema now chronicling Sachsenhausen's devastating past. They can be found on either side of the parade ground where morning roll call was taken and prisoners were forced to watch executions on the gallows.

Next to the cinema is a prison and the bleak remains of what is left of the Station Z extermination block. A map allows visitors to trace the path of new arrivals depending on whether they were to be killed or used as slave labour.

Despite the enlightened Germany of today, a few people still try to forget the past. In 1992, some buildings here were burnt to the ground by locals. Be sure to hire an English audio guide, since all labellings are in German only.

ℹ️ KZ Sachsenhausen Strasse der Nationen 22, Oranienburg

📞 03301 8037 1517

🕐 Apr–Sept, Tues–Sun 8:30am–6:00pm; Oct–Mar, Tues–Sun 8:30am–4:30pm

💶 Admission Free

HOW TO GET THERE

Take the S1 S-Bahn line to Oranienburg. The journey time is approximately 40 minutes from the city centre. Follow the signs to Gedenkstätte Sachsenhausen. The walk should be about 20 minutes once you reach the S-Bahn station.

Travel the world with

PAM ANN

Prepare for take-off with two **free** guides, covering
14 **European** and **long haul** destinations: *Sydney t*
Sitges, America to *Amsterdam, Berlin* to *Barcelona.*

Including Pam's **hot tips** on:

- ✈ Sight seeing and gay nightlife
- ✈ Crucial web sites and the local low-down
- ✈ Health care and the E111 insurance scheme
- ✈ Taking HIV drugs abroad
- ✈ Local sexual health services

Charity no. 28852

The guides are free in selected gay bars, or by calling THT Direct on **0845 12 21 200** or email your postal address to **info@tht.org.uk**

Sam says ...

"Condoms? Buy BEFORE you fly"

eastside

pension · guesthouse

www.eastside-pension.de
tel. (030) 43 73 54 86

Gallery and guesthouse

Checking In

Berlin has a wealth of accommodation options for everyone from the barefoot backpacker to the barefoot Contessa. Prices range wildly but you pretty much get what you pay for. Bargains are a bit hard to come by for five-star rooms and the best finds are often the little boutique properties scattered throughout the city. So if you've got anything from €10 to €1000 at your disposal, you'll be sure to find something to suit your tastes and budget.

The Best Beds

Adlon Hotel Kempinski Berlin

🛈 Unter den Linden 77, Mitte   ☎ 22610   www.hotel-adlon.de
🚇 S-Bahn Unter den Linden   🌀 ③   V, MC, AmEx, DC

The ritziest hotel in town, the Adlon has been the address of choice for Berlin's elite since its opening in 1907. The property now standing on the Unter den Linden isn't the original – that little bit of history burnt down shortly after World War II – instead it's a brand-spanking new whiz-bang piece of ostentation owned and operated by the Kempinski Hotel Group. Staff can be a bit holier than thou if you aren't anyone of note, so my advice is to check out the interiors and sup in the restaurant while leaving the actual rooms to moneyed show-offs.

Art Hotel-Connection Berlin

🛈 Fuggerstrasse 33, Schöneberg   ☎ 2102 1880   www.arthotel-connection.berlin
🚇 U-Bahn Wittenbergplatz   🌀 ①–②   V, MC, AmEx

The most comfortable and convenient gay hotel in Berlin, the Art Hotel-Connection is part of the sprawling Connection/Prinzknecht bar complex that takes up almost an entire city block on Fuggerstrasse. Rooms are quite spacious and the staff go out of their way to keep you informed on gay happenings and nightlife options. Sorry ladies, this one's for gay men only.

CHECKING IN

Bleibtreu

ⓘ Bleibtreustrasse 31, Charlottenburg

☎ 884 740

www.bleibtreu.com

Ⓜ S-Bahn Savignyplatz

Ⓥ ② – ③

V, MC, AmEx, DC

Hotel darling of the media and fashion set, the Bleibtreu is a sleek and chic establishment with a bit of a minimalist feel. A good place to feel hipper than hip (although slightly alienating and cold at times), it's a great place to impress people with your good taste. Rooms are nicely decorated and feature all the amenities you would expect from a property of this calibre – even if they are a little closet-like in terms of size.

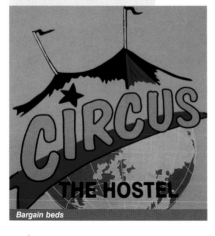

Bargain beds

Circus- The Hostel

ⓘ Rosa-Luxemburg-Strasse 39-41, Mitte

☎ 2839 1433

www.circus-berlin.de

Ⓜ U-Bahn Rosa-Luxemburg-Platz

Ⓥ ① – ②

No credit cards

If you're visiting Berlin on the cheap and don't really care where you rest your head, then the Circus hostel might just be for you. The most popular hostel in town, Circus is a cheery and inexpensive oasis in the often dodgy world of rent-a-beds. The owners are young and hip so they'll know how to cater to your needs. Located a short walk away from the cool-ness that is the Hackescher Markt neighbourhood, it's an extremely convenient jumping-off point. Single-sex rooms are available upon request.

Central location

Crowne Plaza Berlin City Centre

🛈 Nürnburger Strasse 65, Charlottenburg
📞 210 070   http://berlincitycenter.-crowneplaza.com
Ⓤ U-Bahn/S-Bahn Zoologischer Garten
🏳️ ❶–❷–❸ V, MC, AmEx, DC

Normally Crowne Plaza hotels are featureless complexes designed for business people and suburban families. This particular property doesn't sway much from this concept, except for a few key areas. Staff are friendly, facilities are top-notch (including a weight-room, swimming pool and sauna) and the rooms are nicely designed in relaxing beige tones. So what makes it special? Its location. Five minutes from the shopping of Ku'Damm and the buzzing nightlife of gay Schöneberg, it's a quick stumble from anything you might need. The Crowne Plaza is also a member of the IGLTA so you shouldn't have any problem asking for a double room when you check in with a loved one.

Enjoy B & B

🛈 c/o Mann-O-Meter Bülowstrasse 106, Schöneberg
📞 2362 3610
www.ebab.de
Ⓤ U-Bahn Nollendorfplatz
🏳️ ❶
No credit cards

Men only

If you hate the impersonality of hotels and are looking for something that gives you a little more interaction with gay locals, then why not try a homestay organised through Enjoy B & B? Gay Berlin homeowners register their interest in hosting travellers or renting empty properties out on a short- or long-term basis and Enjoy matches them with hopeful tourists. The only drawbacks to the service are that you never know where the property is going to be situated or how the owners are going to react with you. Offices are located in the Mann-O-Meter building and are staffed throughout the day. Gay men only.

Eastside – gayllery & guesthouse

ⓘ Schönhauser Allee 41, Prenzlauer Berg　🅐 4373 5484　🅧 www.eastside-gayllery.de　🅜 U-Bahn Eberswalder Strasse　🅥🅣　V, MC, AmEx

A nice little guesthouse in the heart of the Prenz'l Berg scene, the Eastside is a bit like a home-away-from-home complete with private baths, TV/VCRs and an adjoining shop selling art, books, videos and gay paraphernalia. You'll be given a warm welcome and a nice cup of steaming coffee when you check in. Sort of like the kind of B & B your mother would manage – if she happened to be a screaming homosexual. Men only.

Splendid views from here

Forum Hotel

ⓘ Alexanderplatz, Mitte
🅐 2389 4333
www.forum-berlin.interconti.com
🅜 U-Bahn/S-Bahn Alexanderplatz
🅥 ❷-❸

A massive skyscraper right on the Alexanderplatz, the Forum is a bit of a package-tourist destination property run by the Intercontinental group. Fixtures and fittings can be a bit on the drab side and the bathroom set-up is one of the weirdest I have ever seen. It can be a bit disconcerting using the toilet facilities while your partner looks at you through the see through stall door. So why stay here? The views. The Forum is one of the tallest buildings in Berlin, you can see for miles from your bedroom window. Make sure to request a room facing Alexanderplatz for the best panoramas.

Propeller Island City Lodge

ⓘ Albrecht-Achilles-Strasse 58, Wilmersdorf www.propeller-island.com
🅐 891 9016　🅧 8:00am–12:00pm only　🅜 U-Bahn Adenauerplatz
🅥🅣　V, MC, AmEx

Propeller Island City wins the award for most unique place to sleep in Berlin. Each room is designed and decorated by artist Lars Strochen in a bizarre mix of styles. One room might take on the look of an Italian Renaissance church – the other could be completely upside down. You just never know what you're going to be given. It can be a bit of a crapshoot as to which room Lars gives you, as some of the rooms are decidedly uncomfortable and a little bizarre – but I think the risk is worth it. Checking in can be somewhat of a feat. Make sure to pre-arrange your reservation and time of arrival or you may find yourself waiting for an eternity outside the locked doors.

Westin Grand

ℹ️ Friedrichstrasse 158–64, Mitte
🅰 20270   www.westin-grand.com
Ⓜ U-Bahn Französische Strasse
Ⓥ ③ V, AmEx, DC

Formerly East Berlin's showpiece property, this elegant hotel sits graciously on buzzy Friedrichstrasse, making it a perfect rest-stop for lovers of high-class fashion and great sightseeing. The interiors can sometimes make you feel like you're trapped in the 60s with their dark woods and muted beiges, but the elegance of the sweeping staircase more than makes up for it. Look closely and you might still be able to make out the tiny holes from recording devices planted by the East German government to spy on some of the hotel's noted former guests.

Elegant living

Sleeping Around

ARTEMISIA

🛈 Brandenburgische Strasse 18, Wilmersdorf

📞 873 8905

www.frauenhotel-berlin.de

🚇 U-Bahn Konstanzer Strasse

💳 ①–②

V, MC, AmEx, DC

The city's only women-only property, its location is a bit out of the way and exterior rather less-than-welcoming. Not exclusively lesbian but popular with the Sapphic set.

BRISTOL HOTEL KEMPINSKI BERLIN

🛈 Kurfürstendamm 27, Charlottenburg

📞 884 340 🚇 U-Bahn Kurfürstendamm

💳 ③

V, MC, AmEx, DC

The fanciest hotel on Kurfürstendamm. A bit "concrete bunker" for my taste, the sight of the cute bellhops in grey trousers that are a little too tight for comfort is a nice distraction.

HOTEL ART NOUVEAU

🛈 Leibnizstrasse 59, Charlottenburg

📞 327 7440

www.hotelartnouveau.de

🚇 U-Bahn Adenauer Platz

💳 ②–③

V, MC, AmEx, DC

A true turn-of-the-20th century find for those wanting quality accommodation in a more boutique-style property. No bells or whistles, just a comfortable and conveniently located room with pretty interiors.

HOTEL GARNI ASKANISCHER HOF

🛈 Kurfürstendamm 53, Charlottenburg

📞 881 8033

www.askanischer-hof.de

🚇 U-Bahn Uhlandstrasse

💳 ②–③

V, MC, AmEx, DC

Popular with theatre luvvies and literary folk, this little gem hasn't changed much since its opening in 1910. Furnished with antiques, it's a boutique property with plenty of "olde worlde" charm.

HOTEL GARNI GENDARM

🛈 Charlottenstrasse 61, Mitte 📞 206 0660

www.hotel-gendarm-berlin.de 💳 ②–③ V, MC, AmEx, DC

Five-star rooms at three-star prices. Well located right next to Gendarmenmarkt. One of Mitte's better well-priced properties.

The ritzy Adlon

SCHALL UND RAUCH

ⓘ Gleimstrasse 23, Prenzlauer Berg

✆ 448 0770

www.schall-und-rauch-berlin.de

Ⓤ U-Bahn/S-Bahn Schönhauser Allee

Ⓥ ①

Another gay guest-house option in Prenz'l Berg. This one features an adjoining café/bar and en-suite bathrooms. Breakfast included. Gay men only.

PENSION LE MOUSTACHE

ⓘ Gartenstrasse 4, Mitte

✆ 281 7277

www.lemoustache.de

Ⓤ U-Bahn Oranienburiener Tor Ⓥ ① Cash only

Gay men only with a decided attraction for the harder set. Small but tidy.

REGENT SCHLOSSHOTEL BERLIN

ⓘ Brahmsstrasse 10, Wilmersdorf ✆ 895 840

www.regenthotels.com

Ⓤ S-Bahn Grunewald

Ⓥ ③ V, MC, AmEx, DC

Karl Lagerfeld designed this sprawling Schloss, suitable only if you're the king of a small European monarchy or well-heeled Emir from the Middle East. Completely inconvenient geographically,

it's a bit of a salute to 80s excess.

ROYAL DORINT AM GENDARMENMARKT

ⓘ Charlottenstrasse 50, Mitte ✆ 203 750

www.dorint.de

Ⓤ U-Bahn Stadtmitte

Ⓥ ③

V, MC, AmEx, DC

Foreigners may not know of this beautiful property, but locals certainly do. Almost always full, its popularity is cemented due to its great location, smart interiors and gorgeous health spa complete with plunge pool. Book early to avoid disappoint-ment.

TOM'S HOUSE

ⓘ Eisenacher Strasse 10, Schöneberg ✆ 218 5544

Ⓤ U-Bahn Nollendorfplatz

Ⓥ ① – ②

V, MC, AmEx, DC

If you couldn't get a room at Art Hotel-Connection, give Tom's House a try. Seven double rooms and a lowly single cater to a gay male clientele. Great breakfast–brunches are optional.

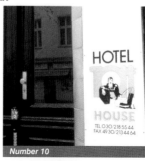

Number 10

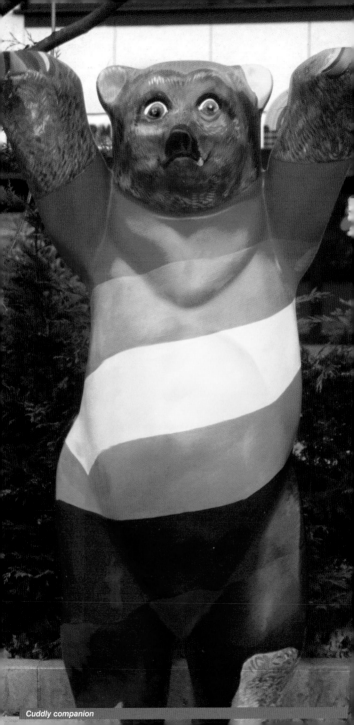

Cuddly companion

out AROUND

Check This Out

Okay, so you've read all the fun stuff and are now booking your trip. This is the section of nitty-gritty details that helps you with all the forward planning and gives you essential information. Be sure to examine it closely if you want to avoid being bearish in Berlin.

Getting There

BY AIR

Surprisingly, Berlin is not a major European gateway city. A lot of this has to do with the fact that it was divided for so long and airport services are struggling to catch up. A vast, new international airport, called Brandenburg International, is scheduled to open within the next decade. Situated where Schönefeld airport currently sits, Brandenburg will increase Schönefeld's capacity immensely and force the closure of the two inner-city airports, Tegel and Tempelhof. Until that time, your airline options will be limited – especially if you are American. Please note that there is no non-stop service from the USA to Berlin. You will have to fly a European carrier and connect in order to reach Berlin as a final destination.

FROM THE UK AND IRELAND
TO/FROM SCHÖNEFELD
BUZZ

0870 240 7070

www.buzzaway.com

TO/FROM TEGEL
BRITISH AIRWAYS

All enquiries 0845 773 3377
www.ba.com

LUFTHANSA

All Irish and UK enquiries
0845 773 7747 www.lufthansa.com

TO/FROM TEMPELHOF
EUROWINGS

0845 773 7747
www.eurowings.de

FROM THE UNITED STATES
AIR FRANCE (VIA PARIS)

1-800-237-2747
www.airfrance.com

BRITISH AIRWAYS (VIA LONDON)

1-800-AIRWAYS
www.britishairways.com

KLM (VIA AMSTERDAM)

1-800-225-2525
www.klm.com

CHECK THIS OUT

LUFTHANSA (VIA FRANKFURT OR MUNICH)
📞 1-800-645-3880
www.lufthansa.com

FROM AUSTRALIA AND NEW ZEALAND

BRITISH AIRWAYS
📞 02/8904-8800 (Australia)
📞 09/356 8980 (New Zealand)

AIR NEW ZEALAND/LUFTHANSA
📞 0800 737 000 (New Zealand)
www.airnewzealand.co.nz www.klmuk.co.uk
📞 1-300-303-747 (Australia)
www.klm.com

AIRPORTS

SCHÖNEFELD AIRPORT
ℹ️ 18 km southeast of the city centre
📞 0180 5000 186
www.berlin-airport.de

Soon to become the main airline hub of Berlin and set to have a name change to the more impressive-sounding "Brandenburg International Airport", Schönefeld is a pain-in-the-ass to arrive at or depart from. Until the launch of its new-fangled replacement, Schönefeld will serve mostly charter and Third World carriers in its tiny confines. Getting to or from Berlin can become a journey in itself, involving buses, trains and your own two feet, so be sure to pack light if landing here. The most efficient way of reaching the downtown core is to take the S-Bahn shuttle bus to S-Bahnhof Flughafen Schönefeld train station and board the Airport Express train that runs from platform seven to Mitte and Zoo every half hour. The

really lazy could take a taxi but will be expected to part with about €35-40 at the end of their journey. The taxi ride takes approximately 45-60 minutes depending on traffic.

TEGEL AIRPORT
ℹ️ 8 km north-west of Mitte
📞 0180 5000 186
www.berlin-airport.de

Until Brandenburg International opens, chances are you'll land at Tegel. A monument to 1970s style, it's a compact airport consisting of the usual facilities and basic souvenir shops – and not much else. Most of the major European carriers land here.

Buses 109 and X9 run directly from the airport to Kurfürstendamm costing €2.10 for the 40-minute journey. If Mitte is your final destination, take the JetExpressBus TXL directly to the Brandenburg Gate, Potsdamer Platz, Französische Strasse U-Bahn or Alexanderplatz. A one-way ticket is €4.10. Taxis run about €20 to anywhere central.

TEMPELHOF AIRPORT
ℹ️ 4 km south of Mitte
📞 0180 5000 186
www.berlin-airport.de

If at all possible, land at Tempelhof. Not only is it the closest airport to the centre of town, but it also has its own U-Bahn station, making it the easiest airport to get to and from. Very few airlines actually fly to Tempelhof anymore, but it's worth looking into, if ease and convenience are a priority. To get away, walk the five-minute jaunt to Platz der Luftbrücke station located just outside the main entrance. A taxi will cost about €14 to Mitte, although you really shouldn't bother taking one unless you absolutely have to.

BY TRAIN

BAHNHOF ZOO
01805 99 66 33
www.bahn.de
U-Bahn/S-Bahn Zoologischer Garten
V, MC, DC, AmEx

The main station for all points west, including Paris, Amsterdam, Brussels and Köln.

BAHNHOF LICHTENBERG
01805 99 66 33
www.bahn.de
U-Bahn/S-Bahn Lichtenberg
V, MC, DC, AmEx

The main terminus for all trains from the south and east, including Vienna, Warsaw, Budapest, Prague and Dresden. Both stations will be replaced in 2006 when the Lehrter Stadtbahnhof is completed north of Tiergarten.

BY BUS
Zentraler Omnibus Bahnhof (ZOB)
Masurenallee 4–6, Charlottenburg
301 0380
U-Bahn Kaiserdamm/S-Bahn Witzleben

The central bus station for all inter-European and domestic coaches. Located opposite the Funkturm and International Congress Centrum.

Tram travel

PASSPORTS AND VISAS

Residents of the EU, Canada, Australia, New Zealand and the United States do not require a visa for any visit to Germany lasting up to three months. A passport, valid for at least three months, is all that is required to enter the country. Other foreign nationals should apply for visas through the German Embassy in their country of origin. Stays of longer than three months require a residence permit regardless of where you come from.

CUSTOMS

EU nationals over the age of 17 years may import limitless goods of a personal nature. Non-EU citizens may only bring in 200 cigarettes or 50 cigars or 250 grams of tobacco, 2 litres of non-sparkling wine plus one litre of spirits or 2 litres of fortified wine, 50g of perfume and any other goods to a value of €175. The import of meat, meat products, fruits, plants, flowers, and protected animals is forbidden. This means you can forget about bringing in any sausage casings to make your own German *bratwurst*.

HIV-positive travellers should have no problem entering the country and do not need to declare their status to any immigration officials.

In The City

TOURIST OFFICE AND INFORMATION

Berlin has a wonderfully complete tourist office staffed with English-speakers galore. A privately run

Lots to do, lots to see

organisation, its website is particularly useful and packed with upcoming events, dates and celebrations. A second branch is open at Brandenburg Gate from 9:30am–9:00pm daily.

ℹ️ Berlin Tourismus Marketing
Europa-Center, Budapester Strasse, Charlottenburg

📞 01805 754 040 www.btm.de

⏱️ Hours: Mon–Sat 8:00am–7:00pm; Sun 9:00am–6:00pm

🚇 U-Bahn/S-Bahn Zoologischer Garten

PUBLIC TRANSPORT

On a map, Berlin looks compact and easily walkable. Think again. Berlin is extremely spread out with each neighbourhood or district taking hours to cross. To combat the sprawl, Berlin has an amazing public transport system that covers pretty much anywhere you might want to go.

U-BAHN/S-BAHN

Berlin's subway and overground rail system is extensive. The U-Bahn alone has more than 170 stations. The key to remembering which is which is that the U-Bahn is underground and useful for getting around the downtown core while the S-Bahn is above-ground and most practical for longer distances, navigating East Berlin, and for its Ringbahn circling the city. The first trains start just after 4:00am and finish up between midnight and 1:00am. The U1/15 and U9 lines run all night on weekends.

BUSES

Berlin's extensive bus network is mind-boggling and difficult to grasp if you don't speak German. Buses come into their own,

however, at night, when 56 routes whisk late-night revellers throughout the metropolis. Bus stops provide timetables and route maps if you get confused.

TRAMS

A leftover from the days of communism, there are 28 lines in the city, mostly in the eastern half. The main tram terminus is located at Hackescher Markt.

REGIONALBAHN

The suburban rail system that links Berlin with its bedroom communities. The easiest way to get to Potsdam and its various sights.

TICKETS

Berlin's transport system is fully integrated, operating on a three-zone system. All tickets (except for the seven-day or longer Zeitkarten) can be purchased from the yellow or orange machines located in all S-Bahn and U-Bahn stations. Make sure to validate your ticket by getting it stamped in the red or yellow box immediately prior to entering the platform. Single tickets within two zones will set you back €2.10. All three zones cost €2.40, while short-distance (three stops or less on the subway, six stops or less on the bus) tickets cost €1.20. A day-pass covering the city is €6.10 for two zones and €6.30 for three. If staying an extended period of time, invest in a Sieben-Tage-Karte (seven day ticket) for €23–€28 or a Monatskarte (month ticket) for €58–€69.50.

TAXIS

Taxis in Berlin are expensive. If you're used to friendly and

CHECK THIS OUT

Berlin by boat

knowledgeable Black Cabs then you're in for a disappointment. A dilapidated Mercedes is the most common possibility, often stinking of body odour and stale cigarettes. Taxis sit at ranks dotted throughout the city. Hailing one off the street is uncommon except in the wee hours of the morning. The starting price is €2.50, and €1.53 for each subsequent kilometre.

CLIMATE

Berlin has a continental climate, often with massive differences in temperature between summer and winter. May to September is the best time to plan a comfortable vacation, although the crowds will certainly be with you. The height of summer can sometimes bring sweltering heat and humidity. Snowfall in early October isn't uncommon and bone-numbing winds that sweep through the flatlands of the area can keep the city firmly locked inside until the end of April.

TELEPHONING

To phone Berlin from outside Germany, dial your country's international access code (00 from the UK, 011 from the US and Canada, 0011 from Australia), followed by 49 (the code for

Germany), 30 (the code for Berlin) and then the local number.

From Berlin, international calls require 00 (the international dialling code), followed by the country code and area code of your call destination.

To call Berlin from other parts of Germany, dial 030 and then the local number.

INTERNATIONAL DIALLING CODES

- Australia 61;
- New Zealand 64;
- Republic of Ireland 353;
- UK 44;
- US and Canada 1

DIRECTORY ASSISTANCE

- 11837 (English-speakers only)
- 11833 (German)

INTERNATIONAL DIRECTORY ASSISTANCE

- 11834

EMBASSIES AND CONSULATES

All the embassies and consulates listed below can provide assistance with lost passports and emergencies. Lists of recommended English-speaking doctors and lawyers are available should you require them. None of the embassies or consulates can forward you money or financial assistance or spring you from jail if you break the law. They will, however, attempt to assist you in any other way that they can.

AUSTRALIAN EMBASSY

- Friedrichstrasse 200, Mitte
- 880 0880
- Mon–Thurs 8:30am–1:00pm 2:00pm–5:00pm; Fri 8:30am–4:00pm
- U-Bahn Stadtmitte

BRITISH EMBASSY

🛈 Wilhelmstrasse 70–71, Mitte

🌐 204 570

✹ 9:00am–12:00pm 2:00pm–4:00pm
daily 🚇 S-Bahn Unter den Linden

CANADIAN EMBASSY

🛈 Friedrichstrasse 95, 12th Floor, Mitte

🌐 203 120

✹ 8:30am–12:30pm, 1:30pm–5:00pm
🚇 U-Bahn/S-Bahn Friedrichstrasse

IRISH CONSULATE

🛈 Friedrichstrasse 200, Mitte

🌐 220 720 ✹ 9:30am–12:30pm,
2:30pm–4:45pm daily 🚇 U-Bahn
Stadtmitte

NEW ZEALAND EMBASSY

🛈 Atrium Friedrichstrasse,
Friedrichstrasse 60, Mitte

🌐 206 210

✹ Mon–Thur 9:00am–1:00pm,
2:00pm–5:30pm; Fri 9:00am–1:00pm,
2:00pm–4:30pm
🚇 U-Bahn/S-Bahn Friedrichstrasse

US EMBASSY

🛈 Neustädtische Kirchstrasse 4, Mitte

🌐 238 5174

✹ 24hrs daily

🚇 S-Bahn Unter den Linden

POLICE AND CRIME

Crime in Berlin is no worse or better than your average large European city. The central police HQ is at Platz der Luftbrücke 6 in Tempelhof (Tel: 6995).

DRUGS

While no Amsterdam by any means, Berlin is pretty liberal about drug use. Possessing ten grams or less of hash or grass will most likely result in confiscation by the police – but that's about it. Some bars and clubs tolerate drug use, but possession of small amounts of

harder drugs may end in a fine, if not jail.

SAFETY AND SECURITY

Homophobic abuse is rare, but if it is going to happen, it usually occurs in East Berlin or in the more densely populated Turkish neighbourhoods (e.g. Kreuzberg). Cruising is legal, but you have to keep an eye out for marauding groups of skinheads and Turkish teens who sometimes think it's fun to harass gay men in known outdoor sex spots.

Walking at night is relatively safe, but you should stick to well-lit main streets, especially in East Berlin communities.

HEALTH

As with all foreign travel, health insurance is recommended. EU citizens will be covered by the reciprocal agreements in effect. E111 forms are required by Britons, available at all DSS offices. German medical costs are about the same as in the US. Vaccinations are not required to enter Germany unless you are arriving via some African, Asian and/or South American nations. All hospitals have emergency wards open 24hrs daily. Should you fall ill in Germany, but it is not an emergency, you must consult a physician before going to any hospital. Contact the AOK Auslandsschalter for advice and assistance.

AOK AUSLANDSSCHALTER

🛈 Karl-Marx-Allee 3, Mitte

🌐 2531 8184 www.aokberlin.de

✹ 8:00am–2:00pm Mon, Wed;
8:00am–6:00pm Tues, Thurs;
8:00am–12:00pm Fri
🚇 U-Bahn/S-Bahn Alexanderplatz

Travel Tips

Berlin bound? Then check out these travellers' health tips.

IF YOU'RE ILL

British passport holders are entitled to free or reduced cost emergency medical care (including emergency HIV-related treatment). But you may have to pay then claim the money back. Using the E111 scheme will mean quicker access to this health care. Get the form from your post office (they must stamp it too) and take it (and a photocopy) on holiday. One E111 form will cover multiple trips within Europe (you'll only need a new one if you change address). Without an E111 you may face charges. It covers tourists but not those studying or working in Germany.

The E111 only gets you basic treatment and is not an alternative to your own private insurance (which covers things the E111 scheme doesn't, like theft, lost luggage etc.). Travellers wanting insurance that covers HIV-related problems can get details of firms offering that from THT Direct on 0845 12 21 200 (10am–10pm).

No vaccinations are needed for Germany.

For more on health care abroad check out *www.doh.gov.uk/traveladvice/treatment2.htm*

TRAVELLING WITH HIV MEDICATION

There are no travel restrictions for people with HIV visiting Germany as tourists. To avoid raising suspicions with Customs officials it's better to leave medication in its original packaging. A note from your doctor might be useful, explaining the drugs are for a 'chronic infection' (without mentioning HIV).

Suitcases can go missing so medicines are best carried in hand luggage.

CONDOMS

Don't rely on free condoms and lube being available in German gay venues. Take enough of both away with you so you won't be caught unprepared.

CONTACT

For help with HIV or sexual health related issues in Berlin there's Mann-O-Meter at Bulowstrasse 106 (Nollendorf underground station). This gay centre is in the heart of Gay Berlin (Schoeneberg/Motzstrasse), with helpful staff and stacks of local info: open 5pm-10pm. For telephone info dial 216 8008 when calling within Berlin.

HIV AND SAFE SEX

Refreshingly enough, HIV-positive travellers should find Germany a joy to visit with few obstacles impeding a pleasant journey. It is perfectly legal to bring HIV medication into the country and it – along with condoms, dental dams and any other safe-sex paraphernalia you might need – is available from pharmacies in the city should you run out. For other STDs, consult a local physician. Lists of recommended English-speaking doctors are available from your embassy.

BERLINER AIDS-HILFE (BAH)

🛈 Büro 15, Meinekestrasse 12, Wilmersdorf

📞 885 6400 or 19411 (Advice Line)

🕑 Mon–Thurs 12:00pm–6:00pm; Fri 12:00pm–3:00pm

Advice Line is open 24hrs daily

🚇 U-Bahn Kurfürstendamm

GAY GROUPS AND RESOURCES

There are a number of gay groups catering to a variety of special interests throughout the city. Three meeting points that host many social groups are aha, Mann-O-Meter and the Sonntags-Club. All three of these locations are great resources if you are new to the city and looking to get your bearings. Check the noticeboards for events and happenings.

AHA – LESBEN UND SCHWULEN-ZENTRUM

🛈 Mehringdamm 61, 2nd Floor, Kreuzberg

📞 692 3600   www.aha-berlin.de

🕑 Sun 5:00pm–10:00pm

🚇 U-Bahn Mehringdamm

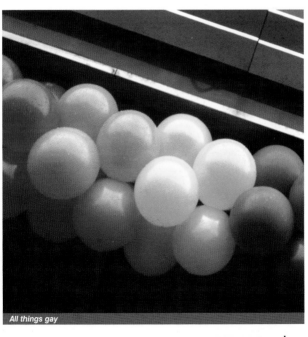

All things gay

CHECK THIS OUT

MANN-O-METER
- Bülowstrasse 106
- 216 8008/216 3336 (emergency)
www.mann-o-meter.de
- Mon-Fri 5:00pm-10:00pm; Sat-Sun 4:00pm-10:00pm
- U-Bahn Nollendorfplatz

SONNTAGS-CLUB
- Greifenhagener Strasse 28
- 449 7590 www.sonntags-club.de
- Hours vary, call ahead
- U-Bahn/S-Bahn Schönhauser Allee

GAY LIFE IN THE CITY

Gay men and lesbians have the same rights as any other citizen in Germany. There are no differences in access to employment or opportunity or adoption. While gay marriage is not legal, legal partnership is – which essentially offers everything marriage offers to hetero couples. The age of consent is standardised for both gays and straights at 14. Police, society and government attitudes towards homosexuality are largely open and tolerant.

MEDIA
GAY PRESS

There are tons of gay publications available in Berlin, but only two (well, one-and-a-half) worth picking up. The Berlin gay bible is *Siegessäule*. Packed with gay and lesbian listings, maps, events and information pages, it's a must for any visitor. Unfortunately, it's only in German. Try and hunt out their English visitors' guide if you have trouble translating.

The other mag worth a look is *Sergej*. More for cute, young gay men, it focuses less on the practical and more on the pretty.

Both publications are free and available at any good gay establish-

ment and at some of the more liberal, hip straight bars around town.

COMMUNICATIONS

Cyber cafés are plentiful. The biggest and best of them is easyInternetCafé located on Kurfürstendamm. It is open 24hrs daily.

The postal service is highly efficient and street-side post boxes are plentiful. Stamps can be purchased from most tobacconists and post offices. Service to the UK takes 3-4 days. Add three more days for post to the US and Canada.

EASYINTERNETCAFÉ
- Kurfürstendamm 224, Charlottenburg
- 8870 7970 www.easyinternetcafe.com
- 24hrs daily
- U-Bahn Kurfürstendamm

MAIN POST OFFICE
- Joachimsthaler Strasse 7, Charlottenburg
- Mon–Sat 8:00am–12:00am
- U-Bahn Kurfürstendamm

CURRENCY, CREDIT CARDS AND BANKS

On 1 January 2002, the currency for Germany became the euro. At time of press, the euro was pretty much on par with the American dollar.

When changing money, try to avoid the conveniently located 24-hour kiosks whose fees and exchange rates aren't competitive. Banks and bureaux de change are usually better, but their commission fees vary.

AMERICAN EXPRESS
- Bayreuther Strasse 37, Schöneberg
- 214 9830 Mon–Fri 9:00am–6:00pm; Sat 10:00am–1:00pm
- U-Bahn Wittenbergplatz

REISEBANK AG

ⓘ Zoo Station, Hardenbergplatz, Charlottenburg

📞 881 7117

🕐 7:30am–10:00pm daily

Ⓤ U-Bahn/S-Bahn Zoologischer Garten

OPENING HOURS

Traditional opening times for banks are 9:00am–12:00pm Monday to Friday and 1:00pm–3:00pm or 2:00pm–6:00pm depending on which branch you hit.

Shops are permitted to stay open until 8:30pm on weekdays and 4:00pm on weekends, but many choose not to. Larger department stores, newsagents and cafés often open earlier and close later. Your best bet for 24hr service is at grocery stores in petrol stations and at *wurst* stalls in centrally located tourist spots. Post offices are open 8:00am–5:00pm during the week and 8:00am–1:00pm Saturdays.

PUBLIC HOLIDAYS AND FESTIVALS

Berlin shuts completely on public holidays. Cafés, restaurants and bars are about the only businesses that stay open – and, boy, do they get packed. Public holidays are: New Year's Day, Good Friday, Easter Monday, May Day/Labour Day (1 May), Ascension Day (7th Sun after Easter), Whit/Pentecost Monday (7th Mon after Easter), Day of German Unity (3 Oct), Day of Prayer and National Repentance (3rd Wed in Nov), Christmas Eve, Christmas Day and Boxing Day (26 Dec). Gay pride events to take note of include: Christopher Street Day Parade (varied Sat in mid–late June), the Love Parade (usually held annually on the 2nd Sat in July) and the Schwul-Lesbisches Strassenfest (2 days in June). They aren't national holidays, but they should be.

TIME

Berlin is on Central European Time, one hour ahead of GMT (Greenwich Mean Time).

ELECTRICITY

German voltage is 220, 50-cycle AC. British appliances should be compatible, but will require an adaptor. Visitors from North America will need to convert their electrical goods or purchase a transformer. German sockets, using a two-pin continental plug, are much larger than American ones.

TIPPING

Tipping is uncommon in Berlin. The standard rule of thumb is to round up to the nearest euro in taxis and give ten percent in restaurants, but this is not obligatory. The words Bediennung Inclusiv on a bill mean that service is included.

Have a great time!

INDEX

INDEX

NOTEBOOK

out AROUND

CONTACT LIST

Name _____

Address _____

_____

_____

Tel _____

Fax _____

email _____

Name _____

Address _____

_____

_____

Tel _____

Fax _____

email _____

Name _____

Address _____

_____

_____

Tel _____

Fax _____

email _____

Name _____

Address _____

_____

_____

Tel _____

Fax _____

email _____

Name _____

Address _____

_____

_____

Tel _____

Fax _____

email _____

Name _____

Address _____

_____

_____

Tel _____

Fax _____

email _____

CONTACT LIST

Name _____

Address _____

_____

_____

Tel _____

Fax _____

email _____

Name _____

Address _____

_____

_____

Tel _____

Fax _____

email _____

Name _____

Address _____

_____

_____

Tel _____

Fax _____

email _____

Name _____

Address _____

_____

_____

Tel _____

Fax _____

email _____

Name _____

Address _____

_____

_____

Tel _____

Fax _____

email _____

Name _____

Address _____

_____

_____

Tel _____

Fax _____

email _____

out AROUND

CONTACT LIST

Name _____

Address _____

_____

_____

Tel _____

Fax _____

email _____

Name _____

Address _____

_____

_____

Tel _____

Fax _____

email _____

Name _____

Address _____

_____

_____

Tel _____

Fax _____

email _____

Name _____

Address _____

_____

_____

Tel _____

Fax _____

email _____

Name _____

Address _____

_____

_____

Tel _____

Fax _____

email _____

Name _____

Address _____

_____

_____

Tel _____

Fax _____

email _____

MY TOP RESTAURANTS

Fill in details of your favourite restaurants below . . .
Tell us about them by logging on to **www.outaround.com**

Restaurant _____

Contact Details _____

Comments _____

_____

_____

_____

Restaurant _____

Contact Details _____

Comments _____

_____

_____

_____

Restaurant _____

Contact Details _____

Comments _____

_____

_____

_____

My Top Restaurants

MY TOP BARS

Fill in details of your favourite bars below . . .
Tell us about them by logging on to **www.outaround.com**

My Top Bars

Bar

Contact Details

Comments

Bar

Contact Details

Comments

Bar

Contact Details

Comments

MY TOP CLUBS

Fill in details of your favourite clubs below . . .
Tell us about them by logging on to **www.outaround.com**

My Top Clubs

Club

Contact Details

Comments

Club

Contact Details

Comments

Club

Contact Details

Comments

AMSTERDAM

BARCELONA & SITGES

BERLIN

MIAMI

NEW YORK

LONDON

PARIS

**Look for the
Rainbow Spine**

**Your Gay Guide
to the World!**

Thomas Co
Publishi

FEEDBACK FORM

Please help us update future editions by taking part in our reader survey. Every returned form will be acknowledged and to show our appreciation we will send you a voucher entitling you to £1 off your next Out Around guide or any other Thomas Cook guidebook ordered direct from Thomas Cook Publishing. Just take a few minutes to complete this form and return it to us.

Alternatively you can visit www.outaround.com and email us the answers to the questions using the numbers given below.

We'd also be glad to hear of your comments, updates or recommendations on places we cover or you think that we ought to cover.

1   Which Out Around guide did you purchase?

2   Have you purchased other Out Around guides in the series?

☐ Yes   ☐ No   If Yes, please specify

3   Which of the following tempted you into buying your Out Around guide. (Please tick as appropriate)

☐ The price
☐ The rainbow spine
☐ The cover
☐ The fact it was a dedicated gay travel guide
☐ Other

4   Please rate the following features of your 'Out Around guide' for their value to you (circle VU for 'very useful', U for 'useful', NU for 'little or no use')

'A Day Out' features	VU	U	NU
Top Sights	VU	U	NU
Top restaurants and cafés and listings	VU	U	NU
Top shops and listings	VU	U	NU
Top hotels and listings	VU	U	NU
Top clubs and bars and listings	VU	U	NU
Theatre and music venues	VU	U	NU
Gyms and sauna choices	VU	U	NU
Practical information	VU	U	NU

FEEDBACK FORM

Feedback Form

5 How did you book your holiday?

☐ Package deal
☐ Package deal through a gay-specific tour operator
☐ Flight only
☐ Accommodation only
☐ Flight and accommodation booked separately

6 How many people are travelling in your party?

7 Which other cities do you intend to/have travelled to in the next/past 12 months?

Amsterdam	Yes ☐	No ☐
Barcelona	Yes ☐	No ☐
London	Yes ☐	No ☐
Miami	Yes ☐	No ☐
New York	Yes ☐	No ☐
Paris	Yes ☐	No ☐
San Francisco	Yes ☐	No ☐
Other (please specify)		

8 Please tell us about any features that in your opinion could be changed, improved, or added in future editions of the book, or any other comments you would like to make concerning the book:

From time to time we send our readers details of new titles or special offers. Please tick here if you wish your name to be held on our mailing list. (Note: our mailing list is never sold to other companies.) ☐

Please detach or photocopy this page and send it to: The Editor, Out Around, Thomas Cook Publishing, PO Box 227, 19–21 Coningsby Road, Peterborough PE3 8XX, United Kingdom.

9 Your age category

☐ under 21 ☐ 21-30 ☐ 31-40 ☐ 41-50 ☐ 51+

First name (or initials)

Last name

Your full address (Please include postal or zip code)

Your daytime telephone number: